Meet the Yorkshire Terrier

- Yorkshire Terriers are characterized as Toy dogs by the American Kennel Club.

- Yorkshire Terriers are commonly and endearingly referred to as "Yorkies."

- As his name implies, the Yorkshire Terrier is a product of Yorkshire County in northern England.

- Historically, Yorkies were used to catch rats for workers in Yorkshire County clothing mills. It wasn't until later in the nineteenth century that Yorkies were discovered by high society and made companion dogs.

- Because of their terrier blood, Yorkies are extremely energetic, playful and inquisitive.

- The Yorkie's long, silky coat is blue and tan and requires daily brushing and regular grooming.

- Yorkshire Terriers are described as being unafraid, independent and adventurous.

- The Yorkie is not aware of his tiny size, therefore he makes just as good a watch-dog as a giant dog.

- Because they are so small and have such splendid coats, many people tend to spoil their Yorkies profusely.

- Yorkshire Terriers can be considered "lap dogs" and "cuddlers" because they enjoy being with their owners all of the time.

Consulting Editor
Ian Dunbar Ph.D., MRCVS
Featuring Photographs by
Jeannie and Bane Harrison
of Close Encounters of the
Furry Kind

Howell Book House
An Imprint of Macmillan General Reference USA
A Pearson Education Macmillan Company
1633 Broadway
New York, NY 10019

Macmillan Publishing books may be purchased for
business or sales promotional use. For information
please write: Special Markets Department,
Macmillan Publishing USA, 1633 Broadway,
New York, NY 10019.

Library of Congress Cataloging-in-Publication
Data
The essential Yorkshire terrier / consulting edi-
tor, Ian Dunbar ; featuring photographs by
Jeannie and Bane Harrison.
    p. cm.
    Includes bibliographical references and index.
    ISBN 1-58245-073-0
    1. Yorkshire terrier.   I. Dunbar, Ian.
    SF429.Y6E77 1999   99-19604
    636.76—dc21   CIP

Manufactured in the United States of America
10 9 8 7 6 5 4 3

Series Director: Michele Matrisciani
Production Team: Stephanie Mohler, Heather Pope
Book Design: Paul Costello
Cover photo and photos pages 47 and 60 are of
    Ch. Mistangay's "Jamie."

Are You Ready?!

☐ Have you prepared your home
and your family for your new
pet?

☐ Have you gotten the proper
supplies you'll need to care for
your dog?

☐ Have you found a veterinarian
that you (and your dog) are
comfortable with?

☐ Have you thought about how
you want your dog to behave?

☐ Have you arranged your schedule to accommodate your dog's
needs for exercise and attention?

*No matter what stage you're at with
your dog—still thinking about getting one, or he's already part of the
family—this Essential guide will
provide you with the practical information you need to understand and
care for your canine companion. Of
course you're ready—you have this
book!*

ESSENTIAL

Yorkshire Terrier

CHAPTER ONE:

Getting to Know Your Yorkshire Terrier 1

CHAPTER TWO:

Homecoming 7

CHAPTER THREE:

To Good Health 16

CHAPTER FOUR:

Positively Nutritious .38

CHAPTER FIVE:

Putting on the Dog 47

CHAPTER SIX:

Measuring Up 56

CHAPTER SEVEN:

A Matter of Fact 62

CHAPTER EIGHT:

On Good Behavior 68

CHAPTER NINE:

Resources 88

Index 92

The Yorkshire Terrier's Senses

SIGHT

The world is a much bigger place when seen through the eyes of the Yorkshire Terrier. But aside from their view, Yorkies, like all dogs, can detect movement at a greater distance than we can, while they can't see as well up close. They can also see better in less light, but can't distinguish many colors.

SOUND

Yorkies can hear about four times better than we can, and they can hear high-pitched sounds especially well.

TASTE

Yorkshire Terriers have fewer taste buds than we do, so they're more likely to try anything—and usually do, which is why it's important for their owners to monitor their food intake. Dogs are omnivorous, which means they eat meat as well as vegetables.

TOUCH

Yorkies are social animals and love to be petted, groomed and played with.

SMELL

A Yorkie's nose is his greatest sensory organ. A dog's sense of smell is so great he can follow a trail that's weeks old, detect odors diluted to one-millionth the concentration we'd need to notice them, even sniff out a person underwater!

CHAPTER ONE

Getting to Know Your Yorkshire Terrier

At heart, the Yorkie is a scrappy working-class terrier that has had no say in the matter of becoming a lap dog. The typical Yorkie personality easily fills the frame of a dog many times its size. If there's one wrong way to go about living with a Yorkie, it is to treat this tiny Toy like a tiny toy!

WHAT MAKES A YORKIE TICK?

There's no denying that Yorkies are captivating little imps, filled with energy, high spirits and an inexhaustible enthusiasm for life. Yorkies are also smart and easily trained. If yours doesn't seem to be

any of those things, you may be working against, rather than with, the Yorkie's basic nature and temperament.

1

Their tiny size and melt-your-heart expression tend to cause owners to spoil their Yorkshire Terriers.

A Yorkie has the same capacity as the next dog to become spoiled, uncooperative, disagreeable and even aggressive. Obviously a dog so small—and Yorkie puppies are very small—needs to be protected from potential hazards and handled gently (more about this in later chapters). Aside from some health and safety considerations, you'll be far ahead of the game if you pretend your puppy will grow up to weigh 20 pounds. Then every time you're tempted to treat her like an orchid, you'll stop yourself.

Yorkie Character

Inasmuch as Yorkies are dogs, they have the full range of canine behaviors. They're social creatures that like to know where they fit in the household "pack." They quickly sort out who belongs and who doesn't; they will bark at strangers; they'll be friendly and outgoing or unfriendly and aloof (largely based on how you train them to be); and of course they chew and dig and scratch and groom themselves in front of company. Yorkie owners sometimes forget that their pets speak dog, not English, which means you have to learn how to communicate with them, not the other way around.

It's also important to realize that every dog is an individual. Some parts of a dog's temperament are inherited from his parents, and while not typical (not what the standard calls for), a few individual Yorkies may be timid or nervous rather than bold. Puppies whose first weeks aren't spent in a loving home with a conscientious breeder may get a bad start in life that will show up as atypical temperament and behavior; these characteristics can sometimes be overcome, but sometimes they can't. Fortunately, the vast majority of Yorkies does seem to be just what the standard calls for: confident, vigorous and self-important. The following are some of the distinctive qualities that are likely to show up in your dog.

Tenacity

Yorkies have astonishing drive and stick-to-it-ive-ness, which are, of course, hunting attributes. Why, then, do we often hear that they're willful and stubborn? In truth, willfulness and perseverance are really

These Yorkies demonstrate the playful, fun-loving side inherent to the breed.

the same qualities—the only difference is whether the task at hand is performed at your encouragement or to your dismay. Take a Yorkie into the ordinary, repetitive obedience training class, for example, and you'll see willfulness as art form; give your Yorkie something intrinsically interesting to do, such as chase and retrieve a small floppy object that lends itself to a good shaking, and you'll lose count of the number of times he'll want to play this "game."

Tenacity is most likely to show up when the Yorkie is in his "hunting" mode. Never mind that the prey is a knotted sock or a favorite

This little tike thinks he's a big dog and will instinctively protect his friends and family from danger.

ball that has rolled out of reach under a table. The Yorkie may well take up a day-long vigil, ignoring repeated calls to dinner and other favorite activities. A bit of Milk Bone can set the Yorkie off on a three-hour search for the perfect place among the sofa pillows to bury it.

Boldness

Many Yorkie owners tell proud but harrowing tales of the day their little dog took on the rogue Rottweiler down the street, and it's a rare multi-breed home where the top dog is not the Yorkie. However, bold does not mean aggressive. Bold is what you get when you mix great inquisitiveness, or the instinct to protect, with self-confidence.

Whether or not you're amused by your Yorkie's boldness, never lose sight of the fact that he can get into trouble. No matter how large his ego, he is still a little dog that can be seriously injured.

Intelligence

Yorkies are as smart as whips. They do well in sports like obedience and agility that require the dog to carry out a complex series of commands, and where success depends on the ability of the dog and handler to communicate with one another. They can learn to recognize an astonishing number of words, distinguish and fetch separate toys in a box by their names and are generally very rewarding for the teacher who likes an apt pupil.

Yorkies also have an uncanny ability to make complex chains of associations—when there's something in it for them.

Activeness—In Body and Mouth

Most tiny dogs are active and quick and the Yorkie is no exception. Someone used to a St. Bernard would likely be inclined to label a Yorkie as hyperactive. In describing the normally active Yorkie, words like darting, dashing, scampering, hopping and bouncing come to mind. A Yorkie that actually walks on his daily walks is quite likely ancient, ill, too hot or he has been trained to walk that way. Be aware that Yorkies do have a lot to say. It's the terrier in them that prompts the need to bark . . . and bark. On the other hand, when the Yorkie barks, there usually is a reason. Yorkies

make excellent watchdogs. They sleep lightly, awaken in a heartbeat and are in motion (and in voice) in the time it takes a larger, more placid dog to lift its head from the floor. Train your Yorkie when to "bark" and when to "shush" and you'll have the most efficient, and definitely the cutest, burglar alarm money can buy.

Independence

The final Yorkie characteristic may seem inconsistent with the others, but the well-bred, and especially the well-handled, Yorkie can be quite content to be near you without

Energy abounds in the dashing, darting Yorkie. This one is doing the weave poles on an agility course.

After a long day at play, this Yorkie appreciates his rest and relaxation time.

necessarily being on your feet at every moment. Yorkies throw themselves into whatever they do, but their small bodies have small fuel tanks, and they know when they need to rest. At these times, the Yorkie is likely to disappear behind the shoes in your closet or into a warm out-of-the-way corner for some downtime.

A precursor to this characteristic is also found in the Yorkie's ancestry.

Terriers were expected to hunt in the company of handlers or other dogs, but also to have the self-confidence to go out on their own after prey. Owners who are not prepared for their Yorkshire's independence can feel hurt and disappointed. On the other hand, pampered and indulged Yorkies are more likely to be clingy and demanding, while ironically lacking in true terrier self-confidence.

CHAPTER TWO

Homecoming

What an exciting time! A puppy is entering your life, and even more exciting—she's a Yorkshire Terrier, who'll grab your heart as you grab hers. Aware of the responsibility that accompanies her, you're prepared, long before her arrival, with all of her needs. Since her first two weeks in your home will be highly stressful for her (and you), your preparedness will minimize your anxiety and heighten your joyful anticipation.

PUT TO THE TEST

Choosing a puppy is usually a happy expedition to a breeder's home or kennel. Do not be put off if your puppy's owner puts you through the "third degree," asking questions like, "Where will the puppy sleep? Where will the puppy stay while you're at work? Do you have a fenced-in yard? If you owned a dog before, what happened to her?" All

It is important to understand the special needs of puppies before you bring yours home.

This puppy's homecoming was a big event in her life, but proper preparation by her owner made the transition a stress-free one.

don't be afraid to ask the breeders questions about prospective puppy's early socialization and training to try and determine whether their puppy is a suitable choice for your home.

Picking Your Puppy

We shall assume you pass the "test" easily. Now, which puppy in the litter will be yours? The breeder may offer you a choice of only one or two. That's perfectly all right. There are very likely to be "reservations" for one or more of the babies—people who left deposits even before birth. Excellent breeders are

of these questions are designed to determine whether yours is a suitable home for the sweet puppy. But sometimes booked well in advance of whelping.

If you do have a choice, be sure to pick a lively, alert animal, one that bounces up to greet you and wants to interact with the family. Do not be taken by the shy, shivering pup in the corner, no matter how "sorry" you may feel for her. Remember—she was raised under the same conditions as her littermates, and for reasons unknown to you, has not developed into a happy, well-adjusted animal. This could be temporary, due to a curable illness, or it could be genetic, meaning that she may grow to be an unhappy adult.

Before bringing home your new family member, do a little planning to help make the transition easier. The first decision to make is where the puppy will live. Will she have access to the entire house or be limited to certain rooms? A similar consideration applies to the yard. It is simpler to control a puppy's activities and to housetrain the puppy if she is confined to definite areas. If doors do not exist where needed, baby gates make satisfactory temporary barriers. Your puppy's long term confinement area (a single room such as a bathroom or kitchen or

exercise pen) should contain a comfortable bed, an adequate supply of clean, fresh water, several stuffed, clean toys and a doggy toilet.

Make sure your Yorkie will have company and companionship during the day. If the members of your family are not at home during the day, try to come home at lunch time, let your puppy out and spend some time with her. If this isn't possible, try to get a neighbor or friend who lives close by to come spend time with the puppy. Your Yorkie thrives on human attention and guidance, and a puppy left alone most of the day will find ways to get your attention, most of them not so cute and many downright destructive.

Yorkie puppies are very social and shouldn't be left alone for long periods of time.

for a while, a *small* crate is not advisable. Never lock a young puppy in a small crate for more than one hour, let alone an entire day—you will force her to soil her sleeping area, and this puppy will now be a dickens of a job to housetrain.

One of the most important things to take care of before you bring your new Yorkie home is selecting a veterinarian to whose care you'll entrust your puppy. You can rely on the recommendations of dog-owning friends, or other knowledgeable sources. After your puppy's arrival (preferably within forty-eight hours), your veterinarian should give her a checkup and vaccination schedule, and answer any questions you may have.

ACCESSORIES

The breeder should tell you what your puppy has been eating. Buy some of this food and have it on hand when your puppy arrives. Keep the puppy on the food and feeding schedule of the breeder, especially for the first few days. If you want to switch foods after that, introduce the new one slowly, gradually adding more and more to the old until it has been entirely replaced.

A dog crate will provide your Yorkie with a quiet, private place to rest or play.

A dog crate is an excellent investment and is an invaluable aid in raising a puppy. It provides a safe, quiet place where a dog can sleep. If it's used properly, a crate helps with housetraining. However, long periods (over one hour during the daytime) of uninterrupted stays are not recommended—especially for young puppies. Unless you have someone at home or can have someone come in a few times a day to let her out to relieve herself and socialize with her

An excellent first collar for a tiny Yorkie puppy is a nylon buckle collar. It is lightweight, inexpensive and comes in a variety of plain and designer colors. Find the correct size by measuring around your puppy's neck, then adding two inches. Expect to replace this collar once or twice as your pup grows; adjustable collars, which "grow" with puppies' necks are generally too bulky for a neck as tiny as a Yorkie's.

In addition to a collar, you'll need a leash. Choose a nylon leash of about the same width as the collar, equipped with a swivel and safety snap. (If you like the look and feel of leather, wait until the puppy is both a little more substantial and is finished teething—roughly 6 months of age. Most leads come in 4-or 6-foot lengths; the shorter size is long enough for the Yorkie. It is important to make sure that the clip on the leash is of excellent quality and cannot become unclasped on its own.

Excessive chewing can be partially resolved by providing a puppy with her own chew toys. Small-size dog biscuits are good for the teeth and also act as an amusing toy. Do not buy chew toys composed of compressed particles, as these particles disintegrate when chewed

PUPPY ESSENTIALS

To prepare yourself and your family for your puppy's homecoming, and to be sure your pup has what she needs, you should obtain the following:

Food and Water Bowls: One for each. We recommend stainless steel or heavy crockery—something solid but easy to clean.

Bed and/or Crate Pad: Something soft, washable and big enough for your soon-to-be-adult dog.

Crate: Make housetraining easier and provide a safe, secure den for your dog with a crate—it only looks like a cage to you!

Toys: As much fun to buy as they are for your pup to play with. Don't overwhelm your puppy with too many toys, though, especially the first few days she's home. And be sure to include something hollow you can stuff with goodies, like a Kong.

I.D. Tag: Inscribed with your name and phone number.

Collar: An adjustable buckle collar is best. Remember, your pup's going to grow fast!

Leash: Style is nice, but durability and your comfort while holding it count, too. You can't go wrong with leather for most dogs.

Grooming Supplies: The proper brushes, special shampoo, toenail clippers, a toothbrush and doggy toothpaste.

11

IDENTIFY YOUR DOG

It is a terrible thing to think about, but your dog could somehow, someday, get lost or stolen. For safety's sake, every dog should wear a buckle collar with an identification tag. A tag is the first thing a stranger will look for on a lost dog. Inscribe the tag with your dog's name and your name and phone number.

There are two ways to permanently identify your dog. The first is a tattoo, placed on the inside of your dog's thigh. The tattoo should be your Social Security number or your dog's AKC registration number. The second is a microchip, a rice-sized pellet that is inserted under the dog's skin at the base of the neck, between the shoulder blades. When a scanner is passed over the dog, it will beep, notifying the person that the dog has a chip. The scanner will then show a code, identifying the dog.

and can get stuck in the puppy's throat. Hard rubber toys are excellent for chewing, as are large rawhide bones. Kongs are especially wonderful since they may be stuffed with a couple of milkbones plus some kibble (part of your Yorkie's daily diet) to encourage chewing. Avoid the smaller chewsticks, as they can splinter and choke the puppy. Anything given to a dog must be large enough that it cannot be swallowed.

The final starter items a puppy will need are a water bowl and food dish. Bowls are available in plastic, stainless steel and even ceramic. Stainless steel is probably the best choice, as it is practically indestructible. Nonspill dishes are available for the dog that likes to play in her water.

PUPPY-PROOFING

Outside

The single best preventive measure one can take to ensure that a dog is not lost or stolen is to provide her with a completely fenced yard. If you have a fence, it should be carefully inspected to ensure there are no holes or gaps in it, and no places where a vigorous and mischievous

Providing your puppy with a collar and ID tag, like the ones worn by this puppy, is the most responsible thing an owner can do for a pet.

This puppy runs free in her fenced-in backyard.

puppy could escape by digging an escape path under the fence.

If you do not have a fenced yard, it would be useful to provide at least an outside kennel area where the puppy could safely relieve herself. Failing that, the youngster should be walked outdoors on a lead several times a day, taking care at first that her collar is sufficiently tight around her neck so that she cannot slip out of it.

Inside

You will also need to puppy-proof your home. Curious puppies will get

Puppy-proofing will protect your Yorkie from getting into things she shouldn't.

HOUSEHOLD DANGERS

Curious puppies and inquisitive dogs get into trouble not because they are bad, but simply because they want to investigate the world around them. It's our job to protect our dogs from harmful substances, like the following:

In the Garage

antifreeze

garden supplies, like snail and slug bait, pesticides, fertilizers, mouse and rat poisons

In the House

cleaners, especially pine oil

perfumes, colognes, aftershaves

medications, vitamins

office and craft supplies

electric cords

· chicken or turkey bones

chocolate, onions

some house and garden plants, like ivy, oleander and poinsettia

into everything everywhere. Even if you generally keep your Yorkie close to you or in her indoor or outdoor enclosure, there will be times when she wants to explore and you cannot watch her. Make sure your home has been puppy-proofed so you can be reasonably confident she won't do serious damage to herself or your home.

Securely stow away all household cleaners and other poisonous products such as antifreeze, slug bait and chocolate which, unfortunately, have a sweet taste dogs seem to love. Remember, the Yorkie is a very small dog and consumption of very small quantities of poison can be fatal. Tobacco products are particularly hazardous.

Keep all electrical cords out of reach, and secure electrical outlets.

Make sure you have removed poisonous plants from your house and garden. Puppies put everything into their mouths, and you need to make sure there's nothing dangerous they can get into. Inside, dangerous plants include poinsettia, ivy and philodendron. Outside, holly, hydrangea and azalea are among the plants of which your puppy should steer clear. The bulbs and root systems of daffodils, tulips and others are also poisonous.

These Yorkie puppies need a regular routine consisting of playing, eating and sleeping.

THE ALL-IMPORTANT ROUTINE

Most puppies do best if their lives follow a schedule. They need definite and regular periods of time for playing, eating and sleeping. Puppies like to start their day early. This is a good time to take a walk or play some games of fetch. After breakfast, most are ready for a nap. How often this pattern is repeated will depend on one's daily routine. Sometimes it is easier for a working person or family to stick with a regular schedule than it is for someone who is home all of the time.

CHAPTER THREE

To Good Health

Today, the owner of a Yorkshire Terrier is truly fortunate, and for many reasons. Given a reasonable

level of consistent, attentive care, most Yorkies will enjoy at least a dozen happy years.

Another reason for the good fortune of today's Yorkie owner is one shared by all dog owners. Modern advances in veterinary science have done for our dogs what advances in human medicine have done for us. Today, your Yorkie can look forward to a lifetime of better health care in both routine and unusual situations.

PREVENTIVE CARE

The easiest way to make sure your Yorkie remains healthy and sound is to make preventive care a priority from the start. This will require a minimal, but essential, amount of effort on your part, and will mean less money in vet bills and less heartache and discomfort for you and your Yorkie later on.

Choose a knowledgeable veterinarian, and establish a good working relationship with him or her. Follow the vaccination schedule you devise with your vet, and be sure to follow up with boosters when necessary. Examine your Yorkie from head to tail everyday (and check for cuts, lumps and parasites) when you groom him.

Keeping your puppy's environment safe and clean will do much to minimize potential hazards. Keep your puppy on a leash or in an enclosed yard, and make sure he has some basic obedience training. This will help to make sure your pup heeds your commands when necessary. If you are trying to call him near a busy street, you need to be reasonably sure he won't tear off into oncoming traffic.

VACCINATIONS

One of the most important items on your agenda on the day you get your new Yorkie puppy is to get a copy of his health records. This will

YOUR PUPPY'S VACCINES

Vaccines are given to prevent your dog from getting infectious diseases like canine distemper or rabies. Vaccines are the ultimate preventive medicine: They're given before your dog ever gets the disease so as to protect him from the disease. That's why it is necessary for your dog to be vaccinated routinely. Puppy vaccines start at 8 weeks of age for the five-in-one DHLPP vaccine and are given every three to four weeks until the puppy is 16 months old. Your veterinarian will put your puppy on a proper schedule and will remind you when to bring in your dog for shots.

include the types and names of all inoculations, and when they were given, as well as a complete list of wormings. Take this to your veterinarian on your first visit, and she or he will set up a schedule to continue these inoculations.

The diseases your puppy needs to be vaccinated against include distemper, hepatitis, parainfluenza and leptospirosis. All the diseases your puppy needs protection from have specific symptoms and means of transmission. Remember all these diseases are extremely serious (most are fatal) and they are all easily preventable with vaccinations.

The veterinarian of your choice should have a good rapport with your Yorkie.

Distemper is a viral disease and is highly contagious and is spread by canine urine and feces An affected dog will run a high fever, cough, vomit, have diarrhea and seizures. These symptoms will worsen, ultimately leading to death.

Hepatitis is a most serious liver disorder characterized by fever, abdominal pain, vomiting and diarrhea.

Parainfluenza, also known as "kennel cough," is not a particularly debilitating upper respiratory infection characterized by a dry, nonproductive cough, but it is extremely infectious. The mode of inoculation for parainfluenza is usually through the nostrils, with a specially adapted syringe tip. Because there are so many strains of this disease (much like the flu in humans), one vaccine cannot prevent them all. However, if you are planning on making any kind of trip to another location or will be boarding your puppy in a kennel facility, a parainfluenza shot is necessary.

Leptospirosis is a bacterial disease spread by the urine of infected animals. Mice and rats are especially implicated in transmission, so

protection is a good idea. This is
particularly important for Yorkies,
since they will relentlessly seek out
rats and mice in their environment.
Pest control! It's a good idea to
speak to the vet about this vaccination, since leptospirosis shots sometimes result in a bad reaction in the
puppy.

Parvovirus and **coronavirus**
have become noteworthy health
problems among companion dogs.
Both diseases are extremely infectious and spread by canine feces.
Affected dogs show a high fever and
bloody and/or mucoid diarrhea.
Their behavior is lethargic, and they
are in great peril as these dangerous
diseases are often fatal. Happily,
there is protection against both
these killers. Get your puppy inoculated, and keep him away from
sickly-looking dogs or places where
many dogs congregate. Parvovirus in
particular is extremely hardy and
may survive in the environment for
many months.

Dog owners are required by law
to have their pets inoculated for
rabies. This disease is characterized
by altered behavior; shy animals may
appear friendly or aggressive. As the
virus spreads, the animal will begin
to salivate excessively and drool. The

PREVENTIVE CARE PAYS

Using common sense, paying attention to your
dog and working with your veterinarian, you
can minimize health risks and problems. Use
vet-recommended flea, tick and heartworm
preventive medications; feed a nutritious diet
appropriate for your dog's size, age and activity
level; give your dog sufficient exercise and regular grooming; train and socialize your dog;
keep current on your dog's shots; and enjoy all
the years you have with your friend.

*No owner
would want to
deprive this
precious pup of
preventive care.*

virus is spread through the animal's
saliva. There is no cure for rabies in
dogs. People who have been bitten
by a rabid animal must endure a
long and painful series of shots. This

This Yorkie is monitored often for signs of illness.

is one vaccine that is not optional, with good reason!

Booster Shots

After your puppy gets his first permanent shot, he should have an annual booster. Always keep your Yorkie's shots current. You open a door to disaster for your pet when you let boosters slide.

INTERNAL PARASITES

There's no getting away from it—worms are a fact of life, but you can do a lot to make sure they don't cause problems for your Yorkie.

When you pick up your puppy, you should be given, along with the vaccination schedule, the dates of the puppy's previous wormings and the names of the drugs that were used. When you take your new puppy to the veterinarian for that first checkup, take his medical history, and take along a stool sample as well. The veterinarian will examine it and determine what kind of worms, if any, are present. She or he will also give you the appropriate medicine and instruct you on the dosage.

In most cases, worming a puppy is a pretty straightforward matter, and today's medications are much easier on a puppy's delicate system than were the remedies of years ago. Don't ignore a worm infestation, but know that such conditions are not unusual and will respond to proper treatment.

Roundworm

These worms are extremely common and can infest even unborn puppies, passing through the placenta to establish themselves. In heavy infestations, it is not unusual to see live roundworms in a puppy stool.

Roundworms can even be vomited up. They get their name from their tendency to curl up when exposed to air. Symptoms of roundworm infestation include a pot belly and a dull coat. Diarrhea and vomiting are other clues to the presence of these worms. Your veterinarian can dispense the right drugs to expel the pests, and you will probably need to repeat the dosage about ten days later to break the worm's life cycle and get rid of worms that matured after your initial dosing. For puppies, roundworms can be especially serious, so if your puppy has them, act fast.

Tapeworm

Tapeworm is another common internal parasite and is usually spread by fleas, which act as intermediate hosts. A dog troubled with a flea infestation may swallow some fleas while biting at itchy flea bites, and in the process ingest tapeworm eggs. Tapeworms are long, segmented parasites, and the fresh, moving segments are often plainly visible in a stool. Dried segments stuck to the dog's hair near the anus resemble grains of brown rice. A tapeworm-affected dog may have diarrhea, dry skin or appear underweight. He may bite at his hindquarters or "scoot" them along the ground. Again, follow the veterinarian's directions and remember to treat your dog and household surroundings for fleas.

Hookworm

Hookworm is a common cause of anemia and is particularly devastating to young puppies. The parasite gets a good foothold when hygienic conditions are not observed or when dogs are exposed to contaminated areas. A dog may swallow larvae, or the worm may penetrate the dog's skin. Eggs are identifiable through microscopic examination from a fresh stool sample. Your veterinarian can dispense drugs to combat hookworm, but it is also necessary to keep your surroundings clean and prevent the puppy from contact with feces and other animals.

Common internal parasites (l–r): roundworm, whipworm, tapeworm and hookworm.

21

Whipworm

Suspect whipworm if your dog is passing a watery or mucoid stool, shows weakness, weight loss, general symptoms of anemia or appears to be in overall poor condition. Whipworm is not visible to the naked eye, so determination of infestation is up to your veterinarian and his or her microscope. If your dog does have whipworm, you will probably have to have several stool checks done and institute a regimen of medication prescribed by your veterinarian.

Treating your dog for whipworm, by itself, is not enough. Whipworms, like so many other internal parasites, thrive in and are

contracted from contaminated soil and unsanitary conditions. Sanitation and strict monitoring are important to keeping your dog clear of whipworm and all the other insidious parasites that can infest your dog.

Heartworm

The condition is passed by the bite of a mosquito infected with the heartworm larvae. It may take some time for the symptoms to show, and by the time adult worms take up residence in your dog's heart, heroic measures may be needed to restore a dog's health.

It is far easier and wiser to use preventive measures to protect your Yorkie from heartworm infestation. Your veterinarian will draw a blood sample from your dog at the appropriate time and examine it under a microscope for heartworm microfilaria. In the probable event that your dog is negative for heartworm, your veterinarian will dispense the pills or syrup your dog needs to remain free of the parasite.

Suspect heartworm if your dog exhibits a chronic cough and a general weakness, with an unexplained loss of weight. If your dog tests

This owner knows he can help keep his dog disease-free by keeping vaccinations current.

positive, your veterinarian is the only person qualified to treat him.

Protozoans

Not all internal parasites are worms. Tiny, single-celled organisms called protozoans can also wreak havoc in your Yorkie's internal mechanisms, but effective treatment is available. The most common disorders in dogs caused by protozoans are coccidiosis and giardiasis.

Coccidiosis is generally the result of poor hygienic conditions in the dog's surroundings. The symptoms of this inflammation of the intestinal tract include sometimes bloody diarrhea, a generally poor appearance, cough, runny eyes and nasal and eye discharges. The disease is more serious in puppies, who are less resistant.

Giardiasis comes from drinking water contaminated with the disease-causing organism (usually from streams). Giardia is nicknamed "beaver fever" because the organism is spread by beavers that relieve themselves in lakes and streams. As with coccidiosis, diarrhea—the color of milk chocolate—is the symptom to watch for. A veterinarian must make the definite diagnosis.

ADVANTAGES OF SPAY/NEUTER

The greatest advantage of spaying (for females) or neutering (for males) your dog is that you are guaranteed that your dog will not produce puppies. There are too many puppies already available for too few homes. There are other advantages as well.

Advantages of Spaying
No messy heats.

No "suitors" howling at your windows or waiting in your yard.

No risk of pyometra (disease of the uterus) and decreased incidences of mammary cancer.

Advantages of Neutering
Decreased incidences of fighting, but does not affect the dog's personality.

Decreased roaming in search of bitches in season.

Decreased incidences of many urogenital diseases.

EXTERNAL PARASITES

Fleas

For your Yorkie, a good scratch is one of life's little pleasures. However, if your Yorkie appears to

23

FLEAS AND TICKS

There are so many safe, effective products available now to combat fleas and ticks that—thankfully—they are less of a problem. Prevention is key, however. Ask your veterinarian about starting your puppy on a flea/tick repellant right away. With this, regular grooming and environmental controls, your dog and your home should stay pest-free. Without this attention, you risk infesting your dog and your home, and you're in for an ugly and costly battle to clear up the problem.

be spending a lot of time scratching himself and doing so with a vengeance, you should take a closer look. If your Yorkie's skin looks red and irritated and there are little dark flecks throughout his coat, fleas may have set up housekeeping with your pet as their primary host. Bad news? Absolutely, but there are things you can do about it.

First, treat your dog. He should be dipped and given a good bath with a flea and tick shampoo. Be cautious here as some preparations will turn a Yorkie's coat pink. Luckily, nowadays there are several easy-to-administer systematic treatments (available from your vet), which make your dog flea-free.

Getting the fleas off your Yorkie alone is not enough. You must also treat your home and yard. Destroy any contaminated bedding, and go over the dog's entire environment with a spray or fogger to kill all the fleas. This means outdoors as well as inside the home. And even with all this, you must exercise common sense in other matters regarding flea control.

Ticks

Ticks look like tiny spiders. They attach themselves to a passing dog, suck blood from the dog, mate, and drop off, and the females lay thousands of eggs to begin the life cycle yet again. In the course of feeding, the female, which is much larger than the male, becomes engorged with blood. As with fleas, you must rid your dog and your environment of ticks if your control is to be effective.

Ticks are not as active as fleas, so removing them is a little easier. Gently, but thoroughly comb your dog each time you return home from a walk during tick season. Go over the entire dog with a pair of tweezers; do not attempt to remove ticks with your fingers. Yorkie owners unlucky enough to have to deal with ticks can take comfort from the fact that the white coat makes it easier to find the little vampires. When you find a tick, drip a little alcohol directly on it. The alcohol will asphyxiate the tick, causing it to release its hold. Pull it off with tweezers, and drop the tick into a small cup of alcohol, where it will drown and trouble your dog no more. Diligence is the watchword with tick control. Once you've gotten rid of the ticks, during tick season keep your dog out of those wild, woodsy places where ticks hide, waiting for your unsuspecting Yorkie to come along and be their meal ticket.

Also remember that there are several kinds of ticks, and you should know which species are common to your area. The brown dog tick is probably the most common species, but there is a species that can spread Rocky Mountain Spotted Fever, and the tiny deer tick is the mode of transmission for Lyme disease. Lyme disease, like Spotted Fever, can be passed to humans, so be very careful if you find that your dog has a tick infestation. If your dog appears lame for no known reason, he may have contracted Lyme disease and will require veterinary attention.

In checking your Yorkie for ticks, pay particular attention to the

25

A Yorkie's clear, bright eyes and shiny coat are indicators of his good health.

face, the base of the ears, between the toes and the skin around the rear end—all places ticks seem to congregate.

Lice

Happily, these annoyingly persistent creatures are infrequently encountered in this age of enlightened hygiene. However, any dog can contract lice from any infested animal. Lice cause pronounced itching and are an annoying problem neither your dog nor you need. If your dog is harboring lice, treatment is the same as for fleas—a good bath and a dip that does the job.

Mites

Mites infest different areas of a dog's body. You might say the various species are specialists of a sort.

The **ear mite** (*Otodectes cynotis*) is a common problem for dogs with dropped ears, but even Yorkies with their erect ears can be troubled by them. If your Yorkie seems constantly to be scratching at his ears and if, on examination, you notice a dark, crumbly, malodorous accumulation, your dog has ear mites and

must be treated for them. Your veterinarian can give you medication and instructions for clearing up the problem.

Scabies, or sarcoptic mange, is yet another condition related to mite infestation. The causative agent, *Sarcoptes scabei,* is a microscopic organism that burrows under the host's skin, causing intense itching and hair loss. This condition can also be passed to humans. Left untreated, it can spread to a dog's entire body.

Demodetic mange is the name of the condition spread by *Demodex canis.* The mite lives in the dog's hair follicles, causing hair loss and red, thickened skin. Eventually pustules form in infected follicles. Diagnosis via skin scrapings is required, and medicated dips are the treatment of choice to destroy these mites.

FIRST AID AND EMERGENCY CARE

Life for our dogs, as for us, always involves uncertainty. That is why you need to have some ability to administer first aid to your dog in the event of a sudden illness or injury.

Muzzling

The first thing you should know how to do is to handle and transport an injured animal safely. A dog in pain is probably not going to recognize his owner or realize that people are trying to help him. In those circumstances, he is likely to bite. The dog in trouble needs to be muzzled.

Transporting Your Dog in an Emergency

An emergency stretcher can be made from a blanket and, depending on the size of the dog, carried by two or more people. An injured dog can also be carried on a rigid board, in a box or wrapped in a towel and carried in a person's arms. Care should be taken, though, that the manner of transport does not exacerbate the dog's original injury.

Shock

If a dog is in shock, keep him as warm and as quiet as possible and get him emergency veterinary attention at once.

Bleeding

If your dog is bleeding, direct pressure is an effective way to staunch the flow. You can fashion a pressure dressing from gauze or some strong fabric. Wrap the area of the wound, applying even pressure as you apply the gauze strips. If you notice tissue swelling below the site of the wound, ease the pressure or, if necessary, remove the bandage altogether. If you have no gauze, use any clean cloth or your hand as a last resort. For arterial bleeding, you will probably need a tourniquet along with the pressure bandage. You may use gauze strips, cloth or any other material that can be wrapped tightly between the wound and the heart to slow the flow of blood. With a tourniquet, you must remember to loosen the pressure about every ten minutes. Get the injured dog to a veterinarian as soon as possible.

Diarrhea

Diarrhea is often the normal result of your dog having eaten something he shouldn't have. However, it can also be the symptom of something more serious, and in young puppies,

27

WHEN TO CALL THE VETERINARIAN

In any emergency situation, you should call your veterinarian immediately. Try to stay calm when you call, and give the vet or the assistant as much information as possible before you leave for the clinic. That way, the staff will be able to take immediate, specific action when you arrive. Emergencies include:

- Bleeding or deep wounds
- Hyperthermia (overheating)
- Shock
- Dehydration
- Abdominal Pain
- Burns
- Fits
- Unconsciousness
- Broken bones
- Paralysis

Call your veterinarian if you suspect any health troubles.

it can cause dehydration quickly. If diarrhea continues for more than twenty-four hours, or if you notice any other symptoms, call your vet immediately.

Broken Bones

With fractures, you must determine how to help the dog without doing more harm than good. The area of the fracture should be immobilized with the use of a splint or a rolled-up magazine secured with gauze or similar material, and the area should be cushioned to support it as much as possible. In compound fractures, the broken bone will pierce the skin; this is more serious than a simple fracture and should be covered in preparation for transfer to a veterinarian. Fractures are very painful, and the injured dog must be handled with great care and probably muzzled for the safety of all who will handle him.

Heatstroke

The Yorkie's system is admirably suited to the cold, but far less efficient in heat. Dogs can die from heatstroke easily. Regardless of the season, a dog showing signs of heat distress—rapid, shallow breathing and a rapid heartbeat—needs to be cooled down immediately. Spraying or soaking the dog with cold water, or pressing an ice bag or freezer pack against the groin, abdomen,

28

anus, neck and forehead are all effective in bringing down the stricken dog's temperature.

Choking

If your Yorkie is choking, you must act quickly to find and dislodge the foreign object after securing the mouth open by inserting a rigid object between the molars on one side. Use your fingers or, very carefully, use long-nosed pliers or a hemostat to withdraw the object. The Heimlich maneuver can also be used for choking dogs; ask your veterinarian to demonstrate how it's done.

Convulsions

Dogs going through convulsions should be cushioned to avoid self-injury, and you must avoid putting a hand near the mouth of a seizuring dog. Such dogs are not likely to swallow their tongues during an episode, but it is a wise idea to have the dog examined by a veterinarian to determine the cause and means of control. Canine convulsions often respond to a drug-based therapy. See your veterinarian as soon as possible to evaluate the problem and begin a course of appropriate medication.

These Yorkies have healthy eating habits, which tells their owner that they are feeling well.

WHAT'S WRONG WITH MY DOG?

We've listed some common conditions of health problems and their possible causes. If any of the following conditions appear serious or persist for more than 24 hours, make an appointment to see your veterinarian immediately.

CONDITIONS	POSSIBLE CAUSES
DIARRHEA	Intestinal upset, typically caused by eating something bad or overeating. Can also be a viral infection, a bad case of nerves or anxiety or a parasite infection. If you see blood in the feces, get to the vet right away.
VOMITING/RETCHING	Dogs regurgitate fairly regularly (bitches for their young), whenever something upsets their stomach, or even out of excitement or anxiety. Often dogs eat grass, which, because it's indigestible in its pure form, irritates their stomachs and causes them to vomit. Getting a good look at *what* your dog vomited can better indicate what's causing it.
COUGHING	Obstruction in the throat; virus (kennel cough); roundworm infestation; congestive heart failure.
RUNNY NOSE	Because dogs don't catch colds like people, a runny nose is a sign of congestion or irritation.
LOSS OF APPETITE	Because most dogs are hearty and regular eaters, a loss of appetite can be your first and most accurate sign of a serious problem.
LOSS OF ENERGY (LETHARGY)	Any number of things could be slowing down your dog, from an infection to internal tumors to overexercise—even overeating.

Lameness

A Yorkie can go lame for a wide variety of reasons. He can cut a pad, pick up a foreign body (like a thorn) or break a nail. All these things will cause lameness. For cuts, clean the area and apply an antiseptic. If the wound is deep, staunch the bleeding

CONDITIONS	POSSIBLE CAUSES
STINKY BREATH	Imagine if you never brushed your teeth! Foul-smelling breath indicates plaque and tartar buildup that could possibly have caused infection. Start brushing your dog's teeth.
LIMPING	This could be caused by something as simple as a hurt or bruised pad, to something as complicated as hip dysplasia, torn ligaments or broken bones.
CONSTANT ITCHING	Probably due to fleas, mites or an allergic reaction to food or environment (your vet will need to help you determine what your dog's allergic to).
RED, INFLAMED, ITCHY SPOTS	Often referred to as "hot spots," these are particularly common on coated breeds. They're caused by a bacterial infection that gets aggravated as the dog licks and bites at the spot.
BALD SPOTS	These are the result of excessive itching or biting at the skin so that the hair follicles are damaged; excessively dry skin; mange; calluses; and even infections. You need to determine what the underlying cause is.
STINKY EARS/HEAD SHAKING	Take a look under your dog's ear flap. Do you see brown, waxy buildup? Clean the ears with something soft and a special cleaner, and don't use cotton swabs or go too deep into the ear canal.
UNUSUAL LUMPS	Could be fatty tissue, could be something serious (infection, trauma, tumor). Don't wait to find out.

31

and get your Yorkie to the vet. Also, for a painful broken nail, visit your veterinarian as soon as possible. He or she will medicate the injury to promote healing. With a broken nail, the vet will trim off as much as possible and cauterize and wrap the dog's paw.

Insect Bites

If your Yorkie is bitten by any sting-ing insect, remove the stinger, apply a baking soda paste to the affected area and stop the swelling and pain with an ice bag or cold pack. It would be a wise idea to run your pet's wounds past your vet to be sure all is well. An antibiotic may be prescribed.

Bee stings are painful, but even more serious is the possibility that your dog is allergic to them. If so, the sting will start to swell immediately. If this happens, get your Yorkie to the vet as soon as possible. He or she will administer an antihistamine or other treatment.

Vomiting

Your dog will regurgitate when he eats something he shouldn't have, and this is usually nothing to worry about. However, if the vomitus looks bloody or otherwise unusual, call your vet immediately. If your dog has been throwing up, you may want to help him along to recovery by

Keeping plants that are non-toxic can mean the difference between life and death to your Yorkie .

feeding a bland diet of moist rice with a little chicken. You may want to add a tablespoon of yogurt to help restore helpful microbes to the digestive tract. If your dog vomits more than once, take him to the veterinarian.

Poisoning

A dog's curiosity will often lead him to eat or lick things he shouldn't. Unfortunately, many substances are poisonous to dogs, including household products, plants or chemicals. Owners must learn to act quickly if poisoning is suspected because the results can be deadly.

HEREDITARY PROBLEMS OF THE YORKSHIRE TERRIER

Every breed of dog has some sort of breed or type-specific disorder. Some breeds are prone to more serious problems than others. However, none of this means that you must forego the pleasure of your chosen breed's companionship.

The Yorkshire Terrier does present a number of health concerns,

POISON ALERT

If your dog has ingested a potentially poisonous substance, waste no time. Call the National Animal Poison Control Center hot line:

(800) 548-2423 ($30 per case) or

(900) 680-0000 ($20 first five minutes; $2.95 each additional minute)

but in general this is a trouble-free breed and most Yorkies live to a ripe old age.

Legg-Perthes' Disease

Legg-Perthes' disease is the necrotic degeneration of the femoral head. In plain English, that means that the head of the femur (the part of the upper hind-leg bone that fits into the pelvis) crumbles from a cutoff in the blood supply. This may be genetically transmitted, or it may be as a result of trauma. There is no documented proof to certify or disprove either claim. Possibly, Legg-Perthes' can come from either cause. In any case, an affected dog will begin to limp and develop progressively less use of the affected leg. Treatment is via surgical removal of the damaged head and a conservative exercise regimen. Recovery is usually complete and rapid.

Legg-Perthes' disease is another condition that does not manifest itself until the puppy is more than 6 or 7 months old, by which time most pet Yorkies will be in their new homes. The puppy's breeder may have had experience with Legg-Perthes', or this may be the first case. Regardless, let the breeder know about it.

Luxating Patella

The patella is the kneecap and, in ordinary circumstances, it slides up and down in front of the knee joint. With a number of small breeds, including Yorkies, it will slide from its normal position toward the inner leg. The most obvious symptom is the onset of limping. A dog may or may not exhibit pain during these episodes. Luxating patella is a recurring condition that could eventually lead to arthritis; the only permanent cure is surgical correction of the affected knee. Sensible weight control and reasonable exercise levels will also benefit the affected individual.

Collapsing Trachea

The walls of the trachea, or windpipe, of many tiny breeds are flaccid and become more so as the dog ages. The first sign of this condition often is an occasional honking cough, especially on exertion, which may become almost constant in later life. Breathing against the obstruction for many years can result in chronic lung disease and other complications. Sometimes the defect can be repaired with surgery and the coughing controlled with cough suppressants. Overweight Yorkies with this defect are likely to suffer more than those that are lean.

Dental Problems

Although some breeders believe that large, strong, tartar-resistant teeth are inherited, the more relevant genetic factor in dental health may be the alignment of the top and bottom jaws and proper placement of teeth in the jaws. Teeth that are crowded together and overlap one another allow food particles and bacteria to collect, eventually causing gum inflammation, loose teeth and infected roots. Yorkies with crowded teeth should have some of

34

them removed by a veterinarian. Natural healers advocate the use of herbs, fresh whole foods and plenty of hard items to chew in order to promote strong teeth and gums.

Portosystemic Shunt

This is a congenital malformation of the portal vein which brings blood to the liver for cleansing. The presence of a shunt means that blood either partially or completely bypasses the liver, and the "dirty" blood goes on to poison the heart, brain, lungs and other organs. Symptoms vary widely and can include poor appetite, occasional vomiting and diarrhea, poor coordination, decreased ability to learn, seizures (especially after eating), blindness, coma and death. Diagnosing portosystemic shunt is difficult but necessary, as the only cure is surgery. Not all shunts can be repaired, but early treatment offers the best hope of success.

Progressive Retinal Atrophy (PRA)

PRA is a gradual degeneration of the retina in the eye leading to blindness. Onset of the condition in Yorkies usually is not until five to seven years of age. The first sign is night blindness or hesitancy to move about normally in a darkened room. At this time, conventional medicine offers no cure, nor is there a test that can predict which puppies will develop the disease. There is anecdotal evidence that homeopathic remedies have been effective in slowing and even reversing the degenerative process in some cases.

WELL-BEING

Aside from the dog's physical needs—a proper and safe shelter, nutritious diet, health care and regular exercise—the Yorkie needs plenty of plain, old-fashioned love. Bringing your Yorkie into the family provides the dog with a sense of security.

CARE OF THE SENIOR CITIZEN

Eventually your wonderful Yorkie is going to get old, as do we all. To ensure that he continues to enjoy a good quality of life, you can and should do a number of things to keep him both comfortable and happy during his senior years.

Your Yorkie is happiest when he is part of a family, enjoying the social inter-actions, nurtur-ing and play.

36

The Yorkie senior citizen will spend more time sleeping. He may not seem be as attentive to your comings and goings as he did when he was younger. He may walk more slowly with a few more halting steps than the hellion of a puppy you remember from a decade ago. However, he is the reason you learned to love Yorkies, and he needs your love and loyalty now even more than he did when he was a puppy.

Make sure his bed is comfortable and located in a draft-free spot. Also remember that a Yorkie is never too old to be a busybody, so keep his bed where he can keep up with

family activity. A small artificial lambskin rug would be especially appreciated on cold nights.

Now is a good time to talk to your veterinarian about your aging Yorkie's diet. Tell the vet what you are feeding when you bring him in for a checkup, and ask his or her advice about changing food.

Carefully monitor your Yorkie and groom him frequently. Just because the blush of youth is no longer upon him, don't neglect his appearance or his hygiene. Watch his teeth and keep them clean. If any appear broken or rot-ten, have them extracted. Your

Yorkie will be happier and healthier as a result.

Make it a point to check your Yorkie's vision and hearing regularly. Cataracts are a common consequence of aging in dogs. Your Yorkie may lose all or part of his vision, but if you have him in familiar surroundings, he will probably get along just fine. Yes, surgery is available to remove cataracts, but you must also consider whether he is a good candidate for surgery and how much risk he will be exposed to as a result of the anesthetic. Again, your veterinarian is the best qualified person to advise you on the best course of action.

A Yorkie that suffers complete or partial hearing loss needs you to protect him whenever he is out of the house. If he can't hear, he is less likely to react to any imminent danger.

EUTHANASIA

Sometimes a well-loved old dog peacefully slips away in his sleep. Often though, an old dog is brought to the veterinarian's office for euthanasia. Euthanasia (painless death) is a prospect every dog owner must face sooner or later.

The time to consider euthanasia for your dog is when his quality of life is no longer sufficient. Many owners are guilty of thinking more of their own feelings than their dogs' when they elect to delay the inevitable. Remember, your Yorkie has a sense of only the present and the past. He lives today and does not have a handle on the future. For him, the end of life holds no terrors. Euthanasia is not painful, but an old dog's confusion can be terribly stressful. When the sedative is administered, show your dog the loyalty he has shown to you. Stay with him. Let yours be the last voice he hears. You'll be doing the right thing, and you owe it to your dog.

ANOTHER YORKIE

If yours was a one-Yorkie household, you will probably want another to fill the empty space left by your old friend. The time to seek a new Yorkie is for you to determine, but it is better to let a little time go by. This way, you give yourself a chance to heal from the loss of your old pet and allow the newcomer to make his own inroads on your heart in his own ways and for his own reasons.

CHAPTER FOUR

Positively Nutritious

The importance of good feeding is obvious, but the rules for maintaining a dog on good food and a sensible feeding regimen are wonderfully simple. It is when dog owners start making up their own rules about feeding that good husbandry can become derailed.

Dog owners take their pets to the veterinarian when they become ill, to the groomer for a special occasion or to a training session when the spirit moves them. However, they feed their pets every single day. What they are fed, when they are fed and how they are fed are of great importance.

Over the course of a dog's life, her nutritional requirements will change just as ours do, and it is important to be aware of those needs ahead of time. If you approach the entire matter of feeding from a commonsense point of view and arm yourself with good information, you can expect that your dog will be properly fed for her entire life.

FEEDING YOUR YORKIE PUPPY

If you are about to get your first Yorkie, you will surely want to know just what to do to make sure you feed her properly. Before you bring her home, ask what she is being fed and when, and stick to the same food and routine after you get her home. Do this for at least the first week or so.

In most cases, the puppy you get will be on three meals a day. Stick to this number of feedings as much as possible. A Yorkie puppy will continue to grow until she is about 9 months old, and it is important to feed with this fact in mind. You may need to change feeding times to accommodate your own lifestyle. No problem. Just make sure that you

GROWTH STAGE FOODS

Once upon a time, there was puppy food and there was adult dog food. Now there are foods for puppies, young adults/active dogs, less active dogs and senior citizens. What's the difference between these foods? They vary by the amounts of nutrients they provide for the dog's growth stage/activity level.

Less active dogs don't need as much protein or fat as growing, active dogs; senior dogs don't need some of the nutrients vital to puppies. By feeding a high-quality food that's appropriate for your dog's age and activity level, you're benefiting your dog and yourself. Feed too much protein to a couch potato and she'll have energy to spare, which means a few more trips around the block will be needed to burn it off. Feed an adult diet to a puppy, and risk growth and development abnormalities that could affect her for a lifetime.

39

ease the puppy into your requirements. Making abrupt changes can be stressful and physically upsetting for the puppy.

The three-meals-a-day routine should be followed until the puppy reaches about 6 months of age. At this point, put her on a morning and an evening meal until she reaches her first birthday. At a year of age, she will do well on one meal a day,

Dog food comes packaged for all ages and stages, so choosing a product is easier for owners.

Yorkies are typically good eaters.

with biscuits in the morning and at bedtime. However, if you prefer to keep your Yorkie on two meals a day, there is no reason not to.

WHAT TO FEED YOUR YORKIE

Today, we and our dogs benefit from extensive research that has been conducted to find the best foods available for routine, day-to-day feeding, as well as foods for growing puppies, geriatrics, dogs with specific health needs and dogs with high levels of activity. The various dog food companies have gone to considerable expense to develop nutritionally complete, correctly balanced diets for all dogs. Feeding the right amount of a high-quality food should suffice. That may, however, be easier said than done, as owners often have an emotional tendency to enhance their pets' food, often to the detriment of the dog (more on this subject later in the chapter).

Dry Food (Kibble)

The basis of your dog's diet should be dry kibble. A high-quality, well-balanced kibble is nutritionally complete and will be relished by your dog under all normal conditions. Most major dog food companies manufacture a special formulation to meet the explosive growth of young puppies. These are highly recommended for daily feeding up to your Yorkie's first birthday. Use the puppy foods. They work! For a mature dog, choose a kibble with a minimum of 20 percent protein. This and other important nutritional information will be on the label.

Many experienced dog keepers are firm believers in feeding dry

TYPES OF FOODS/TREATS

There are three types of commercially available dog food—dry, canned and semimoist—and a huge assortment of treats (lucky dogs!) to feed your dog. Which should you choose?

Dry and canned foods contain similar ingredients. The primary difference between them is their moisture content. The moisture is not just water. It's blood and broth, too, the very things that dogs adore. So while canned food is more palatable, dry food is more economical, convenient and effective in controlling tartar buildup. Most owners feed a 25 percent canned/75 percent dry diet to give their dogs the benefit of both. Just be sure your dog is getting the nutrition she needs (you and your veterinarian can determine this).

Semimoist foods have the flavor dogs love and the convenience owners want. However, they tend to contain excessive amounts of artificial colors and preservatives.

Dog treats come in every size, shape and flavor imaginable, from organic cookies shaped like postmen to beefy chew sticks. Dogs seem to love them all, so enjoy the variety. Just be sure not to overindulge your dog. Factor treats into her regular meal sizes.

41

kibble, or just flavoring it slightly with broth or canned meat to heighten palatability. Others, just as

How Many Meals a Day?

Individual dogs vary in how much they should eat to maintain a desired body weight—not too fat, but not too thin. Puppies need several meals a day, while older dogs may need only one. Determine how much food keeps your adult dog looking and feeling her best. Then decide how many meals you want to feed with that amount. Like us, most dogs love to eat, and offering two meals a day is more enjoyable for them. If you're worried about overfeeding, make sure you measure correctly and abstain from adding tidbits to the meals.

Whether you feed one or two meals, only leave your dog's food out for the amount of time it takes her to eat it—ten minutes, for example. Free-feeding (when food is available any time) and leisurely meals encourage picky eating. Don't worry if your dog doesn't finish all her dinner in the allotted time. She'll learn she should.

42

Your Yorkie should have access to fresh, cool water at all times.

adamantly, insist that the dog is a natural meat eater and her diet should contain significant amounts of fresh or canned meat. Actually, a diet that mixes both meat and kibble is likely to provide your dog with the best features of both foods. If one had to come down on the side of one food or the other, the winner would have to be an all-kibble diet. Studies have shown that dogs raised on all-meat diets often suffer from malnutrition and serious deficiencies, which may cause extreme physically debilitating problems.

Adding Canned Food or Meat

If you decide to add meat to the food, the best choice is beef. It may be freshly cooked, if you like, or canned. There are some very fine canned meats available, and it is a good idea for you to check the label, looking for about 10 percent protein. Chicken is also a good food source and is available in canned form. If you cook any poultry for your Yorkie, bone it carefully. The same is true for fish, which most dogs relish. Cottage cheese is another good protein source, especially for puppies or dogs convalescing from illness.

Water

Besides feeding a high-quality food, you must keep ample clean, fresh water available for your dog at all times. It is vital to do so.

ESTABLISHING A FEEDING SCHEDULE

Establishing a feeding schedule depends on the demands of your own daily routine. Whatever time you decide, feed at the same time every day. Dogs are creatures of habit and are happiest when maintained on a specific schedule. Of course, there will be days when you can't be there to feed your pet at her regular dinner hour. It's okay. An occasional break in the routine is not a disaster, as long as your dog knows that most of the time she will be fed at a set time.

HOW MUCH TO FEED YOUR YORKIE

The amount of food you feed your Yorkie depends on the individual dog: her age, health, stage of life and activity level.

If your Yorkie is very active, she will burn more calories and need

HOW TO READ THE DOG FOOD LABEL

With so many choices on the market, how can you be sure you are feeding the right food to your dog? The information is all there on the label—if you know what you're looking for.

Look for the nutritional claim right up top. Is the food "100 percent nutritionally complete"? If so, it's for nearly all life stages; "growth and maintenance," on the other hand, is for early development; puppy foods are marked as such, as are foods for senior dogs.

Ingredients are listed in descending order by weight. The first three or four ingredients will tell you the bulk of what the food contains. Look for the highest-quality ingredients, like meats and grains, to be among them.

The Guaranteed Analysis tells you what levels of protein, fat, fiber and moisture are in the food, in that order. While these numbers are meaningful, they won't tell you much about the quality of the food. Nutritional value is in the dry matter, not the moisture content.

In many ways, seeing is believing. If your dog has bright eyes, a shiny coat, a good appetite and a good energy level, chances are her diet's fine. Your dog's breeder and your veterinarian are good sources of advice if you're still confused.

To Supplement or Not to Supplement?

If you're feeding your dog a diet that's correct for her developmental stage and she's alert, healthy looking and neither over- nor underweight, you don't need to add supplements. These include table scraps as well as vitamins and minerals. In fact, unless you are a nutrition expert, using food supplements can actually hurt a growing puppy. For example, mixing too much calcium into your dog's food can lead to musculoskeletal disorders. Educating yourself about the quantity of vitamins and minerals your dog needs to be healthy will help you determine what needs to be supplemented. If you have any concerns about the nutritional quality of the food you're feeding, discuss them with your veterinarian.

more food than a house pet that doesn't get extraordinary amounts of exercise. There will be a difference in the eating patterns of a growing puppy and an elderly animal. If your dog is ill or convalescing, her food needs will also differ from the requirements of a healthy animal. Use your own educated judgment.

If a healthy dog cleans her bowl but still appears hungry, she might need a little more to reach the right amount of daily ration. Adjust accordingly.

Another way to determine whether you are feeding the right amount of food is to let the dog's condition tell you. If your dog is healthy but appears thin, you may want to feed a bit more. If the dog looks to be on the plump side, a more restricted diet is in order. If you can't feel your dog's ribs beneath her fur, she's overweight. Weigh your dog, get your vet's advice and start her on a diet right away.

THE PICKY EATER

A healthy dog will eat food when it's offered and most of the time will clean the dish. If you know your Yorkie is healthy, but she consistently refuses to eat the good food you put in front of her, don't get into the habit of pampering her by offering alternative foods. This will only stiffen her resolve. Feed her at the same time and in the same quiet place every day. Leave the food down for five minutes and then remove it entirely, whether she has eaten or not. Don't worry, a healthy dog will eat before she starves.

FEEDING TWO OR MORE DOGS

If you have to feed two or more dogs, crates can be useful. In multiple-dog households, each dog should eat in her own crate—with the door locked. This way, each dog will eat in comfort, without being threatened by another dog in the household. This also helps you monitor how much each dog eats daily. In the absence of separate crates, dogs should be fed where others in the home cannot get at their food.

PEOPLE FOOD

It can be okay to offer human food at times and to add table scraps occasionally to your dog's food, but do it wisely and in moderation. Dogs like carrots, broccoli and other fresh vegetables; some even like fruits. These are okay, as are bits of cooked meat (no bones). And remember all those balanced rations mentioned earlier in this chapter: Quality food made specifically for dog feeding will do a better job of nourishing your pet than treats you may feel good about offering.

FOOD ALLERGIES

If your puppy or dog seems to itch all the time for no apparent reason, she could be allergic to one or more ingredients in her food. This is not uncommon, and it's why many foods contain lamb and rice instead of beef, wheat or soy. Have your dog tested by your veterinarian, and be patient while you strive to identify and eliminate the allergens from your dog's food (or environment).

Feeding your dog table scraps in addition to her regular meals can cause your Yorkie to gain weight and develop bad manners.

45

BONES

On the matter of bones, your Yorkie is infinitely better off without them.

Your pet will let you know if you are feeding her right by the amount of energy she has.

Certain beef bones are safe enough, but others, such as poultry, chop or fish bones, are definitely dangerous and should never be offered. If you need another reason to keep bones away from your Yorkie, think of what a greasy mess a Yorkie that has been playing with a big soup bone can become. If you can't visualize it, trust me—it's not pretty, and there are many safe chewing items you can give your Yorkie that she will enjoy every bit as much. Alternatively, bury the bones in your Yorkie's digging pit—what a delightful surprise!

CHAPTER FIVE

Putting on the Dog

BEGINNING AT THE BEGINNING

If you acquired your pup from a conscientious breeder, undoubtedly he's already been introduced to the basics of being groomed—a little light brushing, having his nails clipped, a bit of scissoring around his ears and feet, maybe even his first bath. Whatever the breeder did or didn't do, the most important aspect was gently initiating the puppy at a very early age to procedures that will become as much a part of his life as eating.

So if your pet has had this exposure, you're ahead of the game. If he hasn't, the time for you to start is now. It doesn't matter that his coat is only an inch long. It's his attitude you're "grooming" at this point. His

GROOMING TOOLS

pin brush	scissors
slicker brush	nail clippers
flea comb	tooth-cleaning equipment
towel	shampoo
mat rake	conditioner
grooming glove	clippers

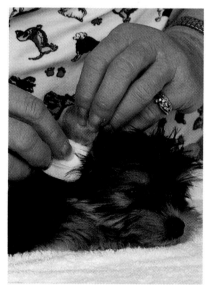

This Yorkie pup was taught early that ear cleaning is nothing to squirm about.

acceptance, your skills and confidence and his coat will all grow together.

As your Yorkie's coat grows, you will need to budget time for grooming; figure an average of ten minutes for this daily task. If you make the mistake of neglecting your daily touch-ups, you will be facing a much larger task on the weekend.

What You'll Need

You don't need a lot of fancy supplies to care for your Yorkie—in the beginning or ever. Down the road, if you find yourself really "getting into" the grooming thing, you may want to invest in additional supplies. For now, the items in the grooming tools sidebar, plus the following additional items should suffice: a sponge, cotton balls, a nonslip mat for the tub, a spray attachment for the faucet, a hair dryer and a baby hair clasp or small rubber bands.

Setting Up

Just as with feeding, walking, training and everything else, you will want to establish a routine for grooming that your puppy can learn to depend on. A good sequence to develop is as follows: brush, comb, trim, bathe, cut nails, blow dry.

But first, where will you do the grooming? Some people train their Yorkies to lay in their laps or on a table for grooming, turning the body from side to side as necessary. Others groom with the dog standing on a stool, table or countertop. Whichever surface you choose, just remember that you cannot take your eyes or hands off the puppy for one single second. Don't even think about whether your dog will jump—he will!

Once you've picked a spot, gather together all your supplies so you can proceed in an orderly way. You don't have to attempt a full-scale grooming session for several weeks. It will pay off in the long run if you start slowly, spend just a few seconds on each maneuver and concentrate on following the same sequence each time.

Tip: Praise him calmly for every few seconds that he is calm and cooperative.

Brushing and Combing

Brush first. This separates the hair, distributes oils and feels good. Then, with short downward strokes, comb slowly and carefully. Begin near the tips of the hair and work your way toward the dog's body, feeling for tangles or small matted areas. If you encounter resistance, stop.

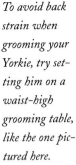

To avoid back strain when grooming your Yorkie, try setting him on a waist-high grooming table, like the one pictured here.

49

With short downward strokes, this woman uses a metal comb on her Yorkie's coat.

This Yorkie is having his foot pad clipped with an electric clipper.

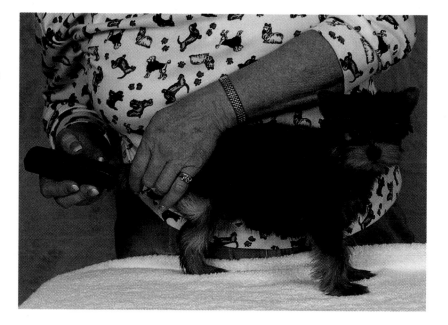

Grasp the problem area with your fingers, lifting the coat to make sure you release any tension against the dog's skin. Then break up the mats with your fingers, the brush or the tip of the comb. Only when you can comb cleanly through the area that was snarled or matted should you release your grip on the coat and comb from the skin outward.

When you're through combing, the comb should run through smoothly, from the skin to the tips of the hair. Not just down the center of his back, but everywhere: in the armpits, on the insides of the rear legs, behind the ears, on the tops of the feet, at the corners of the mouth.

Trimming

There's not much trimming to be done on a Yorkie, and until the hair gets a little longer, you may be snipping air. Still, it's important for both of you to get used to the feel and sound of the scissors and, for some operations, a battery-operated electric clipper. Later on, you may decide you like the look of a "puppy trim," which just means keeping the body coat short and cutting in bangs on the forehead.

FEET—Stand the Yorkie on a table and trim all the way around each foot.

Lift each foot, place the scissors or clipper flat against the pad, and snip any hair that extends beyond the pad (be careful not to pinch the pad as you trim).

EARS—Trim away the hair that grows beyond the edges of the top half of the ear. Don't worry about getting right up to the edge until you're more comfortable. Your Yorkie will be wiggling and tossing his head, but don't try to forcibly restrain him. Concentrate on holding the ear gently but firmly, talking calmly, and going through the motions until he figures out this isn't going to hurt.

ANAL/GENITAL REGION—Your Yorkie will stay cleaner longer if you get in the habit of cutting away the hair that grows around the rectum and genital areas. Practice the motions before you actually cut any hair. Scissoring the genital area is easiest with the dog lying on his back in your lap. Rest one hand on the puppy to steady him—Yorkies are famous for sudden moves.

51

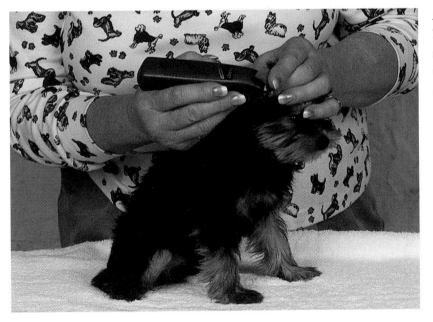

Hold your Yorkie's ear gently but firmly when trimming excess ear hair.

Bathing

Bathe your Yorkie in a warm room, away from drafts. Puppy's first baths will be stressful, so pick a day when nothing else is going on and when the puppy is feeling and eating well. After his bath, your puppy will probably need to urinate, and then want to be left alone for a nice long rest.

Place the nonslip mat in the sink, then cut a hole over the drain so the water can run out. Attach the hose to the faucet and experiment until the temperature is warm and the flow is light to moderate. Put small plugs of cotton in each of your Yorkie's ears, then stand him on the mat in the sink and reassure him for a minute.

Thoroughly wet the coat and the underside of the dog. Use the sponge to wet his head and face. Shampoo the body, add a bit more water, and use your fingers to work up a lather (don't rub the coat in circles). Wash down each leg and under the feet. Wash the head last by applying the shampoo to the sponge. Try to avoid getting shampoo in the eyes or mouth. Then rinse the whole dog thoroughly, first the head, then the body and legs,

Step one: Thoroughly wet your Yorkie's coat with comfortably warm water.

Step two: Apply shampoo and lather.

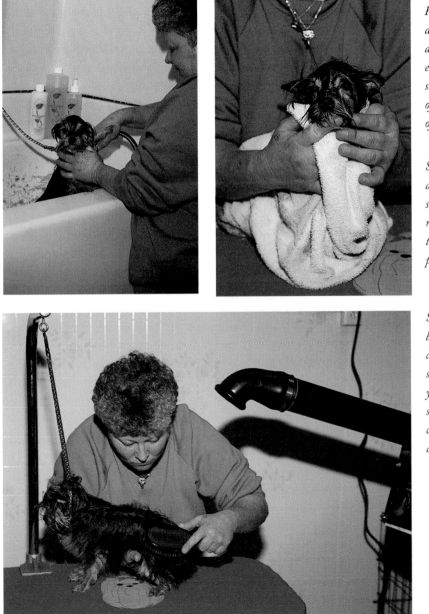

Step three:
Rinse the whole
dog thoroughly
and check that
every speck of
shampoo is out
of the coat and
off the skin.

Step four: Towel
dry your Yorkie,
squeezing as
much water into
the towel as
possible.

53

Step five: Use a
blow dryer on a
comfortable heat
setting, brushing
your Yorkie's
squeaky-clean
coat as it is
dried.

QUICK AND PAINLESS NAIL CLIPPING

This is possible if you make a habit out of handling your dog's feet and giving your dog treats when you do. When it's time to clip nails, go through the same routine, but take your clippers and snip off just the ends of the nail—clip too far down and you'll cut into the "quick," the nerve center, hurting your dog and causing the nail to bleed. Clip two nails a session while you're getting your dog used to the procedure, and you'll soon be doing all four feet quickly and easily.

This owner uses a guillotine nail cutter to trim this Yorkie's nails quickly and painlessly.

then underneath. Make sure every speck of shampoo is out of the coat and off the skin.

Place the puppy on one towel and dry him gently with the other, squeezing as much water as possible into the towel. Now you can scoop him up and dry him with the hair dryer (not too hot and not too close to the skin), brushing his coat as it dries.

Finishing Touches

According to the standard, Yorkies' coats are parted on the face, and from the back of the skull to the end of the tail. Later, you may decide you don't want to be bothered with this, but until then, why not give it a whirl? If your puppy has enough hair for a topknot, comb it up and fasten it in a rubber band or in a clasp. Make sure the hair isn't pulled tight and that you don't accidentally catch any skin in the rubber band. Small ribbons or bits of yarn can be added if you like.

HOW OFTEN?

A stitch in time saves nine, and keeping your Yorkie's coat clean and mat-free is much easier than trying to correct a neglected coat a month later. Here's a recommended schedule:

- Brushing and combing—every day

- Cleaning the beard and under the eyes—every day

- Clipping nails—once a week

- Bathing—once a month or as needed

Some may consider this to be a high-maintenance schedule, but running a comb or brush through a Yorkie's coat can be done anywhere. Try to groom every day while watching television or while hanging out with friends. You will soon find that keeping your Yorkie clean and smooth is not a chore, but another way you can bond with your pet.

Nothing accents a clean and pretty Yorkie like a small ribbon or bow!

55

CHAPTER SIX

Measuring Up

Yorkie! The very name suggests something tiny, cute and perky, and the Yorkshire Terrier is

certainly all of these things. As a well-established purebred dog, the Yorkie's unique physical aspects, or "type," as well as its character traits, are spelled out in a document called the Breed Standard.

The official standard, written by a group of breeders and fanciers known collectively as the Yorkshire Terrier Club of America, and approved by the American Kennel Club, is a kind of blueprint for breeders and judges. The standard ensures that none of the historically important features that characterize the Yorkshire Terrier will be lost in future generations. It is important to remember that a puppy doesn't have to meet the standard in every way to make a suitable pet.

STUDYING THE STANDARD

So how does the standard describe a Yorkshire Terrier? In the following discussion, the sections in italics are taken directly from the standard; the rest is commentary.

General Appearance

That of a long-haired Toy terrier whose blue and tan coat is parted on the face and from the base of the skull to the end of the tail and hangs evenly and quite straight down each side of body. The body is neat, compact and well proportioned. The dog's high head carriage and confident manner should give the appearance of vigor and self-importance.

While the Yorkie's size, coat and color surely are its most unique physical characteristics, it's the terrier in the Yorkie that gives it its "Hey you!" attitude.

HEAD

Small and rather flat on top, the skull not too prominent or round, the muzzle not too long, with the bite neither undershot nor overshot and teeth sound. Either scissors bite or level bite is acceptable. The nose is black. Eyes are

THE AMERICAN KENNEL CLUB

Familiarly referred to as "the AKC," the American Kennel Club is a nonprofit organization devoted to the advancement of purebred dogs. The AKC maintains a registry of recognized breeds and adopts and enforces rules for dog events including shows, obedience trials, field trials, hunting tests, lure coursing, herding, earthdog trials, agility and the Canine Good Citizen program. It is a club of clubs, established in 1884 and composed, today, of over 500 autonomous dog clubs throughout the United States. Each club is represented by a delegate; the delegates make up the legislative body of the AKC, voting on rules and electing directors. The American Kennel Club maintains the Stud Book, the record of every dog ever registered with the AKC, and publishes a variety of materials on purebred dogs, including a monthly magazine, books and numerous educational pamphlets. For more information, contact the AKC at the address listed in Chapter 9, "Resources."

medium in size and not too prominent; dark in color and sparkling with a sharp, intelligent expression. Eye rims are dark. Ears are small, V-shaped, carried erect and set not too far apart.

If the human eye is pleased by balance and symmetry, the Yorkie is a sight for sore eyes indeed. The small head is in proportion with the

Those who love Yorkies love the complete package: tiny size, glossy good looks, keen intelligence and big-dog outlook on life.

A Yorkie's eyes are dark and sparkle with intelligence.

compact body; the little prick ears on one end complement the docked tail on the other. With the whole package draped in steel-blue silk, the Yorkie looks like it belongs on the knee of a monarch.

The physical features that do the most to make up the typical look of the Yorkie are her eyes and ears. Yorkie eyes are dark, and they sparkle with intelligence; her small, erect and mobile ears are like radar dishes that telegraph the Yorkie's lively interest in everything around her. Although the ears are tipped over in very young puppies, they should stand erect by the time the dog is about 3 months old; the Yorkie without fully erect ears will never have typical Yorkie expression. Overall, the expression of the breed is alert, inquisitive and self-confident.

BODY
Well proportioned and very compact. The back is rather short, the back line level, with height at shoulder the same as at the rump.

CHEST AND LEGS
A bright, rich tan, not extending above the elbow on the forelegs nor above the stifle on the hind legs.

LEGS AND FEET

*Forelegs should be straight, elbows nei-
ther in nor out. Hind legs straight
when viewed from behind, but stifles
are moderately bent when viewed from
the sides. Feet are round with black
toenails. Dewclaws, if any, are generally removed from the hind legs.
Dewclaws on the forelegs may be
removed.*

TAIL

*Docked to a medium length and carried
slightly higher than the level of the
back.*

WEIGHT

Must not exceed seven pounds.

The standard states that the
Yorkie is compact and well proportioned. Underneath its very long
coat, its crowning glory, the Yorkie's
body is athletic and sturdy, designed
for a long, active life. Important
physical features are its short, level
back (hips and shoulders are the
same height) and its straight legs
with moderately bent stifles (knees).
The Yorkie also has a moderately
long neck (important for carrying
the head high) and enough forechest
(the part that sticks out in front of
the legs when viewed from the side)
to house a good set of lungs for

WHAT IS A BREED STANDARD?

A breed standard—a detailed description of an
individual breed—is meant to portray the
ideal specimen of that breed. This includes ideal
structure, temperament, gait, type—all aspects
of the dog. Because the standard describes an
ideal specimen, it isn't based on any particular
dog. It is a concept against which judges com-
pare actual dogs and breeders strive to produce
dogs. At a dog show, the dog that wins is the
one that comes closest, in the judge's opinion,
to the standard for its breed. Breed standards
are written by the breed parent clubs, the national organizations formed to oversee the well-
being of the breed. They are voted on and
approved by the members of the parent clubs.

*When full
grown, these lit-
tle ones should
only weigh up to
7 pounds.*

stamina. When trotting along on a loose lead, the Yorkie has a free, jaunty gait, with both head and tail held high. In the Yorkie, small does not mean frail or fragile.

It's important for all Yorkies, whether show or companion quality, to have these basic physical features. Along with health and conditioning, it's a dog's underlying structure that determines the kinds of activities, or lifestyle, it can engage in. In the Yorkie's case, this includes at the very least long walks, preferably where there are squirrels to chase, a brisk game of catch in the backyard

and a spirited session of "tug" in the living room. But it can also include organized all-weather dog sports such as obedience, tracking and agility, which many owners think are too rigorous for small dogs. This is nonsense. A well-built Yorkie is able to do just about anything that a larger dog can do, simply on a "shorter" scale.

COAT

Quality, texture and quantity of coat are of prime importance. Hair is glossy, fine and silky in texture. Coat on the body is moderately long and perfectly straight (not wavy). It may be trimmed to floor length to give ease of movement and a neater appearance, if desired. The fall on the head is long, tied with one bow in center of head or parted in the middle and tied with two bows. Hair on muzzle is very long. Hair should be trimmed short on tops of ears and may be trimmed on feet to give them a neat appearance.

COLORS

Puppies are born black and tan and are normally darker in body color, showing an intermingling of black hair in the tan until they are matured. Color of hair on body and richness of tan on head and legs are of prime importance

This beauty's long muzzle hair and straight, glossy, fine hair blows gracefully in the breeze.

in adult dogs, to which the following
color requirements apply:
BLUE: Is a dark steel-blue, not a
silver-blue and not mingled with
fawn, bronzy or black hairs.
TAN: All tan hair is darker at the roots
than in the middle, shading to still
lighter tan at the tips. There should be
no sooty or black hair intermingled
with any of the tan.

COLOR ON BODY

The blue extends over the body from
back of neck to root of tail. Hair on tail
is a darker blue, especially at end of
tail.

HEADFALL

A rich golden tan, deeper in color at
sides of head, at ear roots and on the
muzzle, with ears a deep rich tan. Tan
color should not extend down on back
of neck.

COMPANION OR SHOW QUALITY?

In simplest terms, the difference
between "show" quality and "companion" quality Yorkies is the extent
to which they meet the standard.
Still, the range of companion or
"pet" quality Yorkies is extremely
broad. It covers everything from a

*Your Yorkie
doesn't measure
up to show qual-
ity? Don't fret.
It's your pup's
capacity to love
you that really
counts!*

well-bred puppy with too many dark
hairs in its tan to be a show dog, to
the sentimental litter out of Aunt
Sally's dog, Freddy, and her next-
door neighbor's dog, Maxine.

But since it is the official standard that describes the ideal
Yorkshire Terrier, and it is only
because of the standard that the
Yorkshire Terrier type has survived
to this day, breeding Yorkies should
be left to those that follow the standard. That means that only a small
percentage of the roughly 38,000
Yorkies registered by the AKC each
year are suitable to be show (and
breeding) stock. But, happily, every
single one of them is suitable to be
the world's best companion to its
owner!

61

CHAPTER SEVEN

A Matter of Fact

If the only Yorkshire Terriers you ever saw were show dogs in full coat and bow-tied topknots, you'd have a hard time imagining how on earth—and why—such a creature

had come into existence. There's no question that today's Yorkie is first and foremost a companion dog. Although all dogs are willing and able to be someone's true-blue pal, few if any breeds were deliberately developed for this reason. If you go far enough back in the history of any pure breed of dogs, you're bound to discover an original utilitarian purpose. The Yorkshire Terrier is no exception.

DOG BREEDING— THEN

In nature, dogs do not vary widely. In different parts of the world, a few basic types evolved from the wolf, in keeping with local climate and terrain. Virtually all of the exaggerated physical characteristics (such as very large or very small size; great coat length or density; and structural extremes such as large heads, flat faces, pendulous ears and elongated bodies) were selected for by man to enhance the dog's usefulness in some way. Likewise, when locally available dogs showed special ability or enthusiasm for specific tasks, people naturally bred these animals to try to "fix" these attributes and pass them on to future generations of puppies. And this is exactly what led to the unique group that includes the Yorkie's forebears.

This Yorkie takes a stroll outdoors, unaware that his ancestors were hardworking dogs that hunted down quarry.

THE TERRIER FACTOR

To understand your Yorkie, you have to understand terriers. What distinguishes the terriers from other kinds of dogs is their strong drive to dig. The word terrier is derived from the French term, *chien terrier*, meaning "dog of the earth." As a hunting group, terriers specialize in pursuing animals (usually vermin rather than game) that live in dens or burrows. Animals that are cornered in their dens, and/or are defending their young, will fight ferociously.

Therefore, any dog that would willingly pursue them had to have an uncommon degree of courage. The kind of dog that most admirably filled the twin bills of small size and large heart was the terrier.

In the field, terriers have been used to drive quarry from its burrow for pursuit by hounds, to hold quarry at bay until hunters with guns could arrive or to dig quarry out and engage it themselves. In many cases, terriers were encouraged to hunt independently, living and dying by their own decisions. Anyone obtaining a terrier needs to know that the wonderful feisty temperament they admire comes with its other, less attractive corollary: independence. To this day terriers are considered hardheaded and difficult to train.

The Legacy of Being Small

The group of dogs called terriers was developed in the fourteenth through nineteenth centuries, mostly in the British Isles. Throughout most of its early history, "Merry Old England" had been a two-class society. The upper classes owned the land and all that grew, lived or moved upon it, and the lower, peasant class owned the shirts on their backs, if they were lucky. At that time, an important source of meat for lordly tables was the furred, feathered and tusked wild game of the forest and field. To help bring down this game, noblemen employed huntsmen, who in turn used large coursing hounds. The peasants, however, were prohibited from taking game from royal forest; the penalty for "stealing" the king's deer, for instance, was hanging. To help enforce the law, peasants were also prohibited from owning any of the large breeds of dogs suitable for hunting. Small dogs, however, were permitted, and there wasn't likely to be much objection if the dogs hunted the small, unsavory varmints that lived below the ground. Thus, the stage was set for a historical association between the poor and a small rugged dog with a strong hunting instinct.

Terriers further developed as specialists in different terrain and for different quarry species. In general, the English Terrier were longer legged, with smooth coats and folded ears, and hunted fox, otter, woodchuck and badger. In contrast, the Scottish Terriers were short-legged, with erect ears and long, harsh coats. They hunted rats, ferrets and weasels as well as rabbits and ground squirrel. It is from the Scottish stock that the Yorkie is descended.

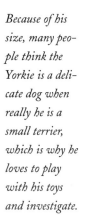

Because of his size, many people think the Yorkie is a delicate dog when really he is a small terrier, which is why he loves to play with his toys and investigate.

MADE IN ENGLAND

As its name implies, the Yorkshire Terrier is a product of Yorkshire County in northern England. By the middle of the nineteenth century, the engine of England's industrial revolution was running full tilt in Yorkshire. In addition to agriculture and livestock production, the area's rich deposits of coal and iron helped fuel the revolution's new industries, including textiles.

In search of work, weavers and other craftsmen had come to Yorkshire from Scotland, bringing with them several different varieties of small long-coated terriers. These so-called Scottish Terriers found ready work themselves in controlling the rodent populations in Yorkshire's mills, mines and factories. On weekends, the dogs' owners were not above a bit of sport, wagering on whose terrier could dispatch the largest number of rats in a given length of time.

While experts are not agreed on exactly which breeds have made up the Yorkshire Terrier, certain breeds are commonly thought to be its main forebears. The possible source of the dog's size, coat length and blue/black color are the Clydesdale,

WHERE DID DOGS COME FROM?

It can be argued that dogs were right there at man's side from the beginning of time. As soon as human beings began to document their existence, the dog was among their drawings and inscriptions. Dogs were not just friends, they served a purpose: There were dogs to hunt birds, pull sleds, herd sheep, burrow after rats—even sit in laps! What your dog was originally bred to do influences the way he behaves. The American Kennel Club recognizes over 140 breeds, and there are hundreds more distinct breeds around the world. To make sense of the breeds, they are grouped according to their size or function. The AKC has seven groups:

1. Sporting
2. Working
3. Herding
4. Hounds
5. Terriers
6. Toys
7. Non Sporting

Can you name a breed from each group? Here's some help: (1) Golden Retriever, (2) Doberman Pinscher, (3) Collie, (4) Beagle, (5) Scottish Terrier, (6) Maltese, and (7) Dalmatian. All modern domestic dogs (*Canis familiaris*) are related, however different they look, and are all descended from *Canis lupus*, the gray wolf.

65

The Yorkshire Terrier's tiny size enabled him to hunt down small varmints that lived below the ground.

66

A terrier that expresses a confident and self-important manner, the Yorkie, was developed in England.

Paisley, Skye and Waterside Terriers, all Scottish breeds brought to England at various points throughout history. Additionally, the English Black and Tan Terrier seems to be the most likely precursor to have lent the Yorkie breed its signature color pattern.

One bit of Yorkie history we do know for sure is that in 1865, in or around the town of Huddersfield, in Yorkshire County, a dog named Ben was born. In his short life (he died of an accident when only 6 years old), he won many prizes at dog shows but also in ratting contests. By today's standards, Ben was a large dog, with only a medium-length coat, no doubt partly due to the active life he led. This dog, known as Huddersfield Ben, is universally acknowledged as the father of the Yorkshire Terrier.

THE YORKIE IN AMERICA

The Yorkie has been a popular breed in the United States since the turn of the century. Yorkies have been entered in shows in America since 1878; the first Yorkie was registered with the AKC in 1885, making it one of the first twenty-five breeds to be approved for registration by the AKC. Yorkies have been in high demand for the ensuing 110 years as one of the most popular Toy breeds and, for the past decade or so, near the top ten of all breeds.

In 1978, a Yorkie won the coveted Best in Show award at the prestigious Westminster Kennel Club show, the first and only member of its breed ever to do so. The dog to win this prize was Champion Cede Higgens, a male dog owned by Charles and Barbara Switzer of Seattle, Washington.

YORKIES AND YOU AND ME

American Yorkies are predominantly house and apartment dogs, often living in multiple-Yorkie households, supporting the idea that if one is good, more are better and many are best! For obvious reasons, Yorkies have great appeal for people with limited space, and because they are small enough to be paper-trained, they are ideal companions for busy people who may get stuck at the office. Still, it's important to remember that your Yorkie is very much a dog that will love to be out and about in the world.

CHAPTER EIGHT

On Good Behavior

by Ian Dunbar, Ph.D., MRCVS

Training is the jewel in the crown—the most important aspect of doggy husbandry. There is no more important variable influencing dog behavior and temperament than the dog's education:

A well-trained, well-behaved and good-natured puppydog is always a joy to live with, but an untrained and uncivilized dog can be a perpetual nightmare. Moreover, deny the dog an education and she will not have the opportunity to fulfill her own canine potential; neither will she have the ability to communicate effectively with her human companions.

Luckily, modern psychological training methods are easy, efficient, effective and, above all, considerably dog-friendly and user-friendly. Doggy education is as simple as it is enjoyable. But before you can have a good time play-training with your new dog, you have to learn what to do and how to do it. There is no bigger variable influencing the success of dog training than the owner's experience and expertise. Before you embark on the dog's education, you must first educate yourself.

BASIC TRAINING FOR OWNERS

Ideally, basic owner training should begin well before you select your dog. Find out all you can about your chosen breed first, then master rudimentary training and handling skills. If you already have your puppydog, owner training is a dire emergency—the clock is ticking! Especially for puppies, the first few weeks at home are the most important and influential days in the dog's life. Indeed, the cause of most adolescent and adult problems may be traced back to the initial days the pup explores her new home. This is the time to establish the *status quo*—to teach the puppydog how you would like her to behave and so prevent otherwise quite predictable problems.

In addition to consulting breeders and breed books such as this one (which understandably have a positive breed bias), seek out as many pet owners with your breed as you

OWNING A PARTY ANIMAL

It's a fact: The more of the world your puppy is exposed to, the more comfortable she'll be in it. Once your puppy's had her shots, start taking her everywhere with you. Encourage friendly interaction with strangers, expose her to different environments (towns, fields, beaches) and most important, enroll her in a puppy class where she'll get to play with other puppies. These simple, fun, shared activities will develop your pup into a confident socialite; reliable around other people and dogs.

can find. Good points are obvious. What you want to find out are the breed-specific problems, so you can nip them in the bud. In particular, you should talk to owners with adolescent dogs and make a list of all anticipated problems. Most important, test drive at least half a dozen adolescent and adult dogs of your breed yourself. An 8-week-old puppy is deceptively easy to handle, but she will acquire adult size, speed and strength in just four months, so you should learn now what to prepare for.

Puppy and pet dog training classes offer a convenient venue to locate pet owners and observe dogs in action. For a list of suitable trainers in your area, contact the Association of Pet Dog Trainers (see chapter 9). You may also begin your basic owner training by observing other owners in class. Watch as many classes and test drive as many dogs as possible. Select an upbeat, dog-friendly, people-friendly, fun-and-games, puppydog pet training class to learn the ropes. Also, watch training videos and read training books. You must find out what to do and how to do it *before* you have to do it.

PRINCIPLES OF TRAINING

Most people think training comprises teaching the dog to do things such as sit, speak and roll over, but even a 4-week-old pup knows how

to do these things already. Instead, the first step in training involves teaching the dog human words for each dog behavior and activity and for each aspect of the dog's environment. That way you, the owner, can more easily participate in the dog's domestic education by directing her to perform specific actions appropriately, that is, at the right time, in the right place and so on. Training opens communication channels, enabling an educated dog to at least understand her owner's requests.

In addition to teaching a dog what we want her to do, it is also necessary to teach her why she should do what we ask. Indeed, 95 percent of training revolves around motivating the dog to want to do what we want. Dogs often understand what their owners want; they just don't see the point of doing it—especially when the owner's repetitively boring and seemingly senseless instructions are totally at odds with much more pressing and exciting doggy distractions. It is not so much the dog that is being stubborn or dominant; rather, it is the owner who has failed to acknowledge the dog's needs and feelings and to approach training from the dog's point of view.

This puppy's first few weeks at home will be the most influ-ential weeks of her life.

This owner directs her Yorkie to sit by using the hand signal for the "sit" command.

The Meaning of Instructions

The secret to successful training is learning how to use training lures to predict or prompt specific behaviors—to coax the dog to do what you want when you want. Any highly valued object (such as a treat or toy) may be used as a lure, which the dog will follow with her eyes and nose. Moving the lure in specific ways entices the dog to move her nose, head and entire body in specific ways. In fact, by learning the art of manipulating various lures, it is possible to teach the dog to assume virtually any body position and

perform any action. Once you have control over the expression of the dog's behaviors and can elicit any body position or behavior at will, you can easily teach the dog to perform on request.

Tell your dog what you want her to do, use a lure to entice her to respond correctly, then profusely praise and maybe reward her once she performs the desired action. For example, verbally request "Fido, sit!" while you move a squeaky toy upwards and backwards over the dog's muzzle (lure-movement and hand signal), smile knowingly as she looks up (to follow the lure) and sits down (as a result of canine

This owner uses her hand as a lure to teach her puppy to walk comfortably on a lead.

anatomical engineering), then praise her to distraction ("Gooood Fido!"). Squeak the toy, offer a training treat and give your dog and yourself a pat on the back.

Being able to elicit desired responses over and over enables the owner to reward the dog over and over. Consequently, the dog begins to think training is fun. For example, the more the dog is rewarded for sitting, the more she enjoys sitting. Eventually the dog comes to realize that, whereas most sitting is appreciated, sitting immediately upon request usually prompts especially enthusiastic praise and a slew of high-level rewards. The dog

begins to sit on cue much of the time, showing that she is starting to grasp the meaning of the owner's verbal request and hand signal.

Why Comply?

Most dogs enjoy initial lure-reward training and are only too happy to comply with their owners' wishes. Unfortunately, repetitive drilling without appreciative feedback tends to diminish the dog's enthusiasm until she eventually fails to see the point of complying anymore. Moreover, as the dog approaches adolescence she becomes more easily distracted as she develops other interests. Lengthy sessions with repetitive exercises tend to bore and demotivate both parties. If it's not fun, the owner doesn't do it and neither does the dog.

Integrate training into your dog's life: The greater number of training sessions each day and the shorter they are, the more willingly compliant your dog will become. Make sure to have a short (just a few seconds) training interlude before every enjoyable canine activity. For example, ask your dog to sit to greet people, to sit before you throw her Frisbee and to sit for her supper.

Really, sitting is no different from a canine "Please." Also, include numerous short training interludes during every enjoyable canine pastime, for example, when playing with the dog or when she is running in the park. In this fashion, doggy distractions may be effectively converted into rewards for training. Just as all games have rules, fun becomes training . . . and training becomes fun.

Eventually, rewards actually become unnecessary to continue motivating your dog. If trained with consideration and kindness, performing the desired behaviors will become self-rewarding and, in a sense, your dog will motivate herself. Just as it is not necessary to reward a human companion during an enjoyable walk in the park, or following a game of tennis, it is hardly necessary to reward our best friend—the dog—for walking by our side or while playing fetch. Human company during enjoyable activities is reward enough for most dogs.

Even though your dog has become self-motivating, it's still good to praise and pet her a lot and offer rewards once in a while, especially for a good job well done. And if for no other reason, praising and

rewarding others is good for the human heart.

Punishment

Without a doubt, lure-reward training is by far the best way to teach: Entice your dog to do what you want and then reward her for doing so. Unfortunately, a human shortcoming is to take the good for granted and to moan and groan at the bad. Specifically, the dog's many good behaviors are ignored while the owner focuses on punishing the dog for making mistakes. In extreme cases, instruction is limited to punishing mistakes made by a

Punishment training only teaches your dog to be sneaky, usually performing the undesirable act behind your back.

FINDING A TRAINER

Have fun with your dog, take a training class! But don't just sign on any dotted line, find a trainer whose approach and style you like and whose students (and their dogs) are really learning. Ask to visit a class to observe a trainer in action. For the names of trainers near you, ask your veterinarian, your pet supply store, your dog-owning neighbors or call (800) PET-DOGS (the Association of Pet Dog Trainers.)

trainee dog, child, employee or husband, even though it has been proven punishment training is notoriously inefficient and ineffective and is decidedly unfriendly and combative. It teaches the dog that training is a drag, almost as quickly as it teaches the dog to dislike her trainer. Why treat our best friends like our worst enemies?

Punishment training is also much more laborious and time consuming. Whereas it takes only a finite amount of time to teach a dog what to chew, for example, it takes much, much longer to punish the dog for each and every mistake. Remember, there is only one right way! So why not teach that right way from the outset?!

To make matters worse, punishment training causes severe lapses in the dog's reliability. Since it is impossible to punish the dog each time she misbehaves, the dog quickly learns to distinguish between those times when she must comply (so as to avoid impending punishment) and those times when she need not comply, because punishment is impossible. Such times include when the dog is off leash and 6 feet away, when the owner is otherwise engaged (talking to a friend, taking a shower, tending to the baby or chatting on the telephone) or when the dog is left at home alone.

Instances of misbehavior will be numerous when the owner is away, because even when the dog complied in the owner's looming presence, she did so unwillingly. The dog was forced to act against her will, rather than molding her will to want to please. Hence, when the owner is absent, not only does the dog know she need not comply, she simply does not want to. Again, the trainee is not a stubborn vindictive beast, but rather the trainer has failed to teach. Punishment training invariably creates unpredictable Jekyll and Hyde behavior.

TRAINER'S TOOLS

Many training books extol the virtues of a vast array of training paraphernalia and electronic and metallic gizmos, most of which are designed for canine restraint, correction and punishment, rather than for actual facilitation of doggy education. In reality, most effective training tools are not found in stores; they come from within ourselves. In addition to a willing dog, all you really need is a functional human brain, gentle hands, a loving heart and a good attitude.

In terms of equipment, all dogs do require a quality buckle collar to sport dog tags and to attach the leash (for safety and to comply with local leash laws). Hollow chew toys (like Kongs or sterilized longbones) and a dog bed or collapsible crate are musts for housetraining. Three additional tools are required:

1. specific lures (training treats and toys) to predict and prompt specific desired behaviors;

2. rewards (praise, affection, training treats and toys) to reinforce for the dog what a lot of fun it all is; and

3. knowledge—how to convert the dog's favorite activities and games (potential distractions to training) into "life-rewards," which may be employed to facilitate training.

The most powerful of these is knowledge. Education is the key! Watch training classes, participate in training classes, watch videos, read books, enjoy play-training with your dog and then your dog will say "Please," and your dog will say "Thank you!"

75

An owner's most essential training tools are loads of patience, a gentle hand and a loving heart.

HOUSETRAINING

If dogs were left to their own devices, certainly they would chew, dig and bark for entertainment and then no doubt highlight a few areas of their living space with sprinkles of urine, in much the same way we decorate by hanging pictures. Consequently, when we ask a dog to live with us, we must teach her *where* she may dig, *where* she may perform her toilet duties, *what* she may chew and *when* she may bark. After all, when left at home alone for many hours, we cannot expect the dog to amuse herself by completing crosswords or watching the soaps on TV!

Also, it would be decidedly unfair to keep the house rules a secret from the dog, and then get angry and punish the poor critter for inevitably transgressing rules she did not even know existed. Remember: Without adequate education and guidance, the dog will be forced to establish her own rules—doggy rules—and most probably will be at odds with the owner's view of domestic living.

Since most problems develop during the first few days the dog is at home, prospective dog owners must be certain they are quite clear about the principles of housetraining *before* they get a dog. Early misbehaviors quickly become established as the *status quo*—becoming firmly entrenched as hard-to-break bad habits, which set the precedent for years to come. Make sure to teach your dog good habits right from the start. Good habits are just as hard to break as bad ones!

Ideally, when a new dog comes home, try to arrange for someone to be present as much as possible during the first few days (for adult dogs) or weeks for puppies. With only a little forethought, it is surprisingly easy to find a puppy sitter, such as a retired person, who would be willing to eat from your refrigerator and watch your television while keeping an eye on the newcomer to encourage the dog to play with chew toys and to ensure she goes outside on a regular basis.

Potty Training

To teach the dog where to relieve herself:

1. never let her make a single mistake;
2. let her know where you want her to go; and

3. handsomely reward her for doing so: "GOOOOOOOD DOG!!!" liver treat, liver treat, liver treat!

Preventing Mistakes

A single mistake is a training disaster, since it heralds many more in future weeks. And each time the dog soils the house, this further reinforces the dog's unfortunate preference for an indoor, carpeted toilet. Do not let an unhousetrained dog have full run of the house.

When you are away from home, or cannot pay full attention, confine the dog to an area where elimination is appropriate, such as an outdoor run or, better still, a small, comfortable indoor kennel with access to an outdoor run. When confined in this manner, most dogs will naturally housetrain themselves.

If that's not possible, confine the dog to an area, such as a utility room, kitchen, basement or garage, where elimination may not be desired in the long run but as an interim measure it is certainly preferable to doing it all around the house. Use newspaper to cover the floor of the dog's day room. The newspaper may be used to

HOUSETRAINING 1-2-3

1. Prevent Mistakes. When you can't supervise your puppy, confine her in a single room or in her crate (but don't leave her for too long!). Puppy-proof the area by laying down newspapers so that if she does make a mistake, it won't matter.

2. Teach Where. Take your puppy to the spot you want her to use every hour.

3. When she goes, praise her profusely and give her three favorite treats.

soak up the urine and to wrap up and dispose of the feces. Once your dog develops a preferred spot for eliminating, it is only necessary to cover that part of the floor with newspaper. The smaller papered area may then be moved (only a little each day) towards the door to the outside. Thus the dog will develop the tendency to go to the door when she needs to relieve herself.

Never confine an unhousetrained dog to a crate for long periods. Doing so would force the dog to soil the crate and ruin its usefulness as an aid for housetraining (see the following discussion).

77

Teaching Where

In order to teach your dog where you would like her to do her business, you have to be there to direct the proceedings—an obvious, yet often neglected, fact of life. In order to be there to teach the dog where to go, you need to know *when* she needs to go. Indeed, the success of housetraining depends on the owner's ability to predict these times. Certainly, a regular feeding schedule will facilitate prediction somewhat, but there is nothing like "loading the deck" and influencing the timing of the outcome yourself!

Whenever you are at home, make sure the dog is under constant supervision and/or confined to a small area. If already well trained, simply instruct the dog to lie down in her bed or basket. Alternatively, confine the dog to a crate (doggy den) or tie-down (a short, 18-inch lead that can be clipped to an eye hook in the baseboard near her bed). Short-term close confinement strongly inhibits urination and defecation, since the dog does not want to soil her sleeping area. Thus, when you release the puppydog each hour, she will definitely need to urinate immediately and defecate every

third or fourth hour. Keep the dog confined to her doggy den and take her to her intended toilet area each hour, every hour and on the hour. When taking your dog outside, instruct her to sit quietly before opening the door—she will soon learn to sit by the door when she needs to go out!

Teaching Why

Being able to predict when the dog needs to go enables the owner to be on the spot to praise and reward the dog. Each hour, hurry the dog to the intended toilet area in the yard, issue the appropriate instruction ("Go pee!" or "Go poop!"), then give the dog three to four minutes to produce. Praise and offer a couple of training treats when successful. The treats are important because many people fail to praise their dogs with feeling . . . and housetraining is hardly the time for understatement. So either loosen up and enthusiastically praise that dog: "Wuzzzer-wuzzer-wuzzer, hooooser good wuffer den? Hoooo went pee for Daddy?" Or say "Good dog!" as best you can and offer the treats for effect.

Following elimination is an ideal time for a spot of play-training in the yard or house. Also, an empty dog may be allowed greater freedom around the house for the next half hour or so, just as long as you keep an eye out to make sure she does not get into other kinds of mischief. If you are preoccupied and cannot pay full attention, confine the dog to her doggy den once more to enjoy a peaceful snooze or to play with her many chew toys.

If your dog does not eliminate within the allotted time outside—no biggie! Back to her doggy den, and then try again after another hour.

As I own large dogs, I always feel more relaxed walking an empty dog, knowing that I will not need to finish our stroll weighted down with bags of feces!

Beware of falling into the trap of walking the dog to get her to elimi-nate. The good ol' dog walk is such an enormous highlight in the dog's life that it represents the single biggest potential reward in domestic dogdom. However, when in a hurry, or during inclement weather, many owners abruptly terminate the walk the moment the dog has done her business. This, in effect, severely punishes the dog for doing the right thing, in the right place at the right time. Consequently, many dogs

This Yorkie has learned to let her owner know when she has to go out.

become strongly inhibited from eliminating outdoors because they know it will signal an abrupt end to an otherwise thoroughly enjoyable walk.

Instead, instruct the dog to relieve herself in the yard prior to going for a walk. If you follow the above instructions, most dogs soon learn to eliminate on cue. As soon as the dog eliminates, praise (and offer a treat or two)—"Good dog! Let's go walkies!" Use the walk as a reward for eliminating in the yard. If the dog does not go, put her back in her doggy den and think about a walk later on. You will find with a "No feces—no walk" policy, your dog will become one of the fastest defecators in the business.

If you do not have a backyard, instruct the dog to eliminate right outside your front door prior to the walk. Not only will this facilitate clean up and disposal of the feces in your own trash can but, also, the walk may again be used as a colossal reward.

CHEWING AND BARKING

Short-term close confinement also teaches the dog that occasional quiet moments are a reality of domestic living. Your puppydog is extremely impressionable during her first few weeks at home. Regular confinement at this time soon exerts a calming influence over the dog's personality. Remember, once the dog is housetrained and calmer, there will be a whole lifetime ahead for the dog to enjoy full run of the house and garden. On the other hand, by letting the newcomer have unrestricted access to the entire household and allowing her to run willy-nilly, she will most certainly

develop a bunch of behavior problems in short order, no doubt necessitating confinement later in life. It would not be fair to remedially restrain and confine a dog you have trained, through neglect, to run free.

When confining the dog, make sure she always has an impressive array of suitable chew toys. Kongs and sterilized longbones (both readily available from pet stores) make the best chew toys, since they are hollow and may be stuffed with treats to heighten the dog's interest. For example, by stuffing the little hole at the top of a Kong with a small piece of freeze-dried liver, the dog will not want to leave it alone.

Remember, treats do not have to be junk food and they certainly should not represent extra calories. Rather, treats should be part of each dog's regular daily diet: Some food may be served in the dog's bowl for breakfast and dinner, some food may be used as training treats, and some food may be used for stuffing chew toys. I regularly stuff my dogs' many Kongs with different shaped biscuits and kibble. The kibble seems to fall out fairly easily, as do the oval-shaped biscuits, thus rewarding the dog instantaneously for checking out the chew toys. The bone-shaped biscuits fall out after a while, rewarding the dog for worrying at the chew toy. But the triangular biscuits never come out. They remain inside the Kong as lures, maintaining the dog's fascination with her chew toy. To further focus the dog's interest, I always make sure to flavor the triangular biscuits by rubbing them with a little cheese or freeze-dried liver.

If stuffed chew toys are reserved especially for times the dog is confined, the puppydog will soon learn to enjoy quiet moments in her doggy den and she will quickly develop a chew-toy habit—a good habit! This is a simple autoshaping process; all the owner has to do is set up the situation and the dog all but trains herself—easy and effective. Even when the dog is given run of the house, her first inclination will be to indulge her rewarding chew-toy habit rather than destroy less-attractive household articles, such as curtains, carpets, chairs and compact disks. Similarly, a chew-toy chewer will be less inclined to scratch and chew herself excessively.

A great way to divert your Yorkie's need to chew up your belongings is to provide her with lots of her own toys.

TOYS THAT EARN THEIR KEEP

To entertain even the most distracted of dogs, while you're home or away, have a selection of the following toys on hand: hollow chew toys (like Kongs, sterilized hollow longbones and cubes or balls that can be stuffed with kibble). Smear peanut butter or honey on the inside of the hollow toy or bone, stuff the bone with kibble and your dog will think of nothing else but working the object to get at the food. Great to take your dog's mind off the fact that you've left the house.

82

Also, if the dog busies herself as a recreational chewer, she will be less inclined to develop into a recreational barker or digger when left at home alone.

Stuff a number of chew toys whenever the dog is left confined and remove the extra-special-tasting treats when you return. Your dog will now amuse herself with her chew toys before falling asleep and then resume playing with her chew toys when she expects you to return. Since most owner-absent misbehavior happens right after you leave and right before your expected return, your puppydog will now be conveniently preoccupied with her chew toys at these times.

COME AND SIT

Most puppies will happily approach virtually anyone, whether called or not; that is, until they collide with adolescence and develop other more important doggy interests, such as sniffing a multiplicity of exquisite odors on the grass. Your mission, Mr./Ms. Owner, is to teach and reward the pup for coming reliably, willingly and happily when called—and you have just three months to get it done. Unless adequately reinforced, your puppy's tendency to approach people will self-destruct by adolescence.

Call your dog ("Fido, come!"), open your arms (and maybe squat down) as a welcoming signal, waggle a treat or toy as a lure and reward the puppydog when she comes running. Do not wait to praise the dog until she reaches you—she may come 95 percent of the way and then run off after some distraction. Instead, praise the dog's first step towards you and continue praising enthusiastically for every step she takes in your direction.

When the rapidly approaching puppy dog is three lengths away from impact, instruct her to sit ("Fido, sit!") and hold the lure in front of you in an outstretched hand to prevent her from hitting you mid-chest and knocking you flat on your back! As Fido decelerates to nose the lure, move the treat upwards and backwards just over her muzzle with an upwards motion of your extended arm (palm-upwards). As the dog looks up to follow the lure, she will sit down (if she jumps up, you are holding the lure too high). Praise the dog for sitting. Move backwards and call her again. Repeat this many times over, always praising when Fido comes and sits; on occasion, reward her.

For the first couple of trials, use a training treat both as a lure to entice the dog to come and sit and as a reward for doing so. Thereafter, try to use different items as lures and rewards. For example, lure the dog with a Kong or Frisbee but reward her with a food treat. Or lure the dog with a food treat but pat her and throw a tennis ball as a reward. After just a few repetitions, dispense with the lures and rewards; the dog will begin to respond willingly to your verbal requests and hand signals just for the prospect of praise from your heart and affection from your hands.

Instruct every family member, friend and visitor how to get the dog to come and sit. Invite people over for a series of pooch parties; do not keep the pup a secret—let other people enjoy this puppy, and let the pup enjoy other people. Puppydog parties are not only fun, they easily attract a lot of people to help you train your dog. Unless you teach your dog how to meet people, that is, to sit for greetings, no doubt the dog will resort to jumping up. Then you and the visitors will get annoyed, and the dog will be punished. This is not fair. Send out those invitations for puppy parties and teach your dog to be mannerly and socially acceptable.

Even though your dog quickly masters obedient recalls in the house, her reliability may falter when playing in the backyard or local park. Ironically, it is the owner who has unintentionally trained the dog not to respond in these instances. By allowing the dog to play and run around and otherwise have a good time, but then to call the dog to put her on leash to take her home, the dog quickly learns playing is fun but training is a drag. Thus, playing in the park becomes a severe distraction, which works against training. Bad news!

Instead, whether playing with the dog off leash or on leash, request her to come at frequent intervals— say, every minute or so. On most occasions, praise and pet the dog for a few seconds while she is sitting, then tell her to go play again. For especially fast recalls, offer a couple of training treats and take the time to praise and pet the dog enthusiastically before releasing her. The dog will learn that coming when called is not necessarily the end of the play session, and neither is it the end of the world; rather, it signals an enjoyable, quality time-out with the owner before resuming play once more. In fact, playing in the park now becomes a very effective life-reward, which works to facilitate training by reinforcing each obedient and timely recall. Good news!

RELEVANCY TRAINING

Once you have taught the dog what you expect her to do when requested to sit, the time is right to teach the dog why she should comply with your wishes. The secret is to have many (many) extremely short training

interludes (two to five seconds each) at numerous (numerous) times during the course of the dog's day. Especially work with the dog immediately before the dog's good times and during the dog's good times. For example, ask your dog to sit and/or lie down each time before opening doors, serving meals, offering treats and tummy rubs; ask the dog to perform a few controlled doggy push-ups before letting her off leash or throwing a tennis ball; and perhaps request the dog to sit-down-sit-stand-down-stand-rollover before inviting her to cuddle on the couch.

Similarly, request the dog to sit many times during play or on walks, and in no time at all the dog will be only too pleased to follow your instructions because she has learned that a compliant response heralds all sorts of goodies. Basically all you are trying to teach the dog is how to say please: "Please throw the tennis ball. Please may I snuggle on the couch."

Remember, it is important to keep training interludes short and to have many short sessions each and every day. The shortest (and most useful) session comprises asking the dog to sit and then go play during a play session. When trained this way, your dog will soon associate training with good times. In fact, the dog may be unable to distinguish between training and good times and, indeed, there should be no distinction. The warped concept that training involves forcing the dog to comply and/or dominating her will is totally at odds with the picture of a truly well-trained dog. In reality, enjoying a game of training with a dog is no different from enjoying a game of backgammon or tennis with a friend; and walking with a dog should be no different from strolling with a spouse, or with buddies on the golf course.

WALK BY YOUR SIDE

Many people attempt to teach a dog to heel by putting her on a leash and physically correcting the dog when she makes mistakes. There are a number of things seriously wrong with this approach, the first being that most people do not want precision heeling; rather, they simply want the dog to follow or walk by their side. Second, when physically restrained during "training," even though the dog may grudgingly mope by your side when "handcuffed" on leash, let's see what

happens when she is off leash. History! The dog is in the next county because she never enjoyed walking with you on leash and you have no control over her off leash. So let's just teach the dog off leash from the outset to want to walk with us. Third, if the dog has not been trained to heel, it is a trifle hasty to think about punishing the poor dog for making mistakes and breaking heeling rules she didn't even know existed. This is simply not fair! Surely, if the dog had been adequately taught how to heel, she would seldom make mistakes and

This well-trained pup walks calmly by her owner's side.

Having a good attitude about training will make training your Yorkie easier on both of you.

hence there would be no need to correct the dog. Remember, each mistake and each correction (punishment) advertise the trainer's inadequacy, not the dog's. The dog is not stubborn, she is not stupid and she is not bad. Even if she were, she would still require training, so let's train her properly.

Let's teach the dog to enjoy following us and to want to walk by our side off leash. Then it will be easier to teach high-precision off-leash heeling patterns if desired.

Before going on outdoor walks, it is necessary to teach the dog not to pull. Then it becomes easy to teach on-leash walking and heeling because the dog already wants to walk with you, she is familiar with the desired walking and heeling positions and she knows not to pull.

FOLLOWING

Start by training your dog to follow you. Many puppies will follow if you simply walk away from them and maybe click your fingers or chuckle. Adult dogs may require additional enticement to stimulate them to follow, such as a training lure or, at the very least, a lively trainer. To teach the dog to follow: (1) keep walking and (2) walk away from the dog. If the dog attempts to lead or lag, change pace; slow down if the dog forges too far ahead, but speed up if she lags too far behind. Say "Steady!" or "Easy!" each time before you slow down and "Quickly!" or "Hustle!" each time before you speed up, and the dog will learn to change pace on cue. If the dog lags or leads too far, or if she wanders right or left, simply walk quickly in the opposite direction and maybe even run away from the dog and hide.

Practicing is a lot of fun; you can set up a course in your home, yard or park to do this. Indoors, entice the dog to follow upstairs, into a bedroom, into the bathroom, downstairs, around the living room couch, zigzagging between dining room chairs and into the kitchen for dinner. Outdoors, get the dog to follow around park benches, trees, shrubs and along walkways and lines in the grass. (For safety outdoors, it is advisable to attach a long line on the dog, but never exert corrective tension on the line.)

Remember, following has a lot to do with attitude—your attitude! Most probably your dog will not want to follow Mr. Grumpy Troll with the personality of wilted lettuce. Lighten up—walk with a jaunty step, whistle a happy tune, sing, skip and tell jokes to your dog and she will be right there by your side.

CHAPTER NINE

Resources

BOOKS

About Yorkshire Terriers

Ackerman, Lowell J. *Dr. Ackerman's Book of the Yorkshire Terrier*. Neptune, NJ: TFH, 1996.

Brearley, Joan McDonald. *Book of the Yorkshire Terrier*. Neptune, NJ: TFH, 1987.

Gordon, Joan B. *The New Complete Yorkshire Terrier*. New York: Howell Book House, 1993.

About Health Care

American Kennel Club. *American Kennel Club Dog Care and Training*. New York: Howell Book House, 1991.

Carlson, Delbert, DVM, and James Giffen, MD. *Dog Owner's Home Veterinary Handbook*. New York: Howell Book House, 1992.

DeBitetto, James, DVM, and Sarah Hodgson. *You & Your Puppy*. New York: Howell Book House, 1995.

Lane, Marion. *The Humane Society of the United States Complete Guide to Dog Care*. New York: Little, Brown & Co., 1998.

McGinnis, Terri. *The Well Dog Book*. New York: Random House, 1991.

Schwartz, Stephanie, DVM. *First Aid for Dogs: An Owner's Guide to a Happy Healthy Pet*. New York: Howell Book House, 1998.

Volhard, Wendy and Kerry L. Brown. *The Holistic Guide for a Healthy Dog*. New York: Howell Book House, 1995.

About Training

Ammen, Amy. *Training in No Time*. New York: Howell Book House, 1995.

Benjamin, Carol Lea. *Mother Knows Best*. New York: Howell Book House, 1985.

Bohnenkamp, Gwen. *Manners for the Modern Dog*. San Francisco: Perfect Paws, 1990.

Dunbar, Ian, Ph.D., MRCVS. *Dr. Dunbar's Good Little Book*. James & Kenneth Publishers, 2140 Shattuck Ave. #2406, Berkeley, CA 94704. (510) 658-8588. Order from Publisher.

Evans, Job Michael. *People, Pooches and Problems.* New York: Howell Book House, 1991.

Palika, Liz. *All Dogs Need Some Training.* New York: Howell Book House, 1997.

Volhard, Jack and Melissa Bartlett. *What All Good Dogs Should Know: The Sensible Way to Train.* New York: Howell Book House, 1991.

About Activities

Hall, Lynn. *Dog Showing for Beginners.* New York: Howell Book House, 1994.

O'Neil, Jackie. *All About Agility.* New York: Howell Book House, 1998.

Simmons-Moake, Jane. *Agility Training, The Fun Sport for All Dogs.* New York: Howell Book House, 1991.

Vanacore, Connie. *Dog Showing: An Owner's Guide.* New York: Howell Book House, 1990.

Volhard, Jack and Wendy. *The Canine Good Citizen.* New York: Howell Book House, 1994.

MAGAZINES

The AKC GAZETTE, The Official Journal for the Sport of Purebred Dogs
American Kennel Club
260 Madison Ave.
New York, NY 10016
www.akc.org

Dog Fancy
Fancy Publications
3 Burroughs
Irvine, CA 92618
(714) 855-8822
http://dogfancy.com

Dog World
Maclean Hunter Publishing Corp.
500 N. Dearborn, Ste. 1100
Chicago, IL 60610
(312) 396-0600
www.dogworldmag.com

PetLife: Your Companion Animal Magazine
Magnolia Media Group
1400 Two Tandy Center
Fort Worth, TX 76102
(800) 767-9377
www.petlifeweb.com

Dog & Kennel
7-L Dundas Circle
Greensboro, NC 27407
(336) 292-4047
www.dogandkennel.com

MORE INFORMATION ABOUT YORKSHIRE TERRIERS

National Breed Club

YORKSHIRE TERRIER CLUB OF AMERICA
Corresponding Secretary:
Mrs. Shirley A. Patterson
2 Chestnut Ct., Star Rt.
Pottstown, PA 19464
Breeder Contact:
Mrs. Shirley A. Patterson
(610) 469-6781

89

Breed Rescue:
Suzette Heider
(407) 725-8821

The Club can send you information on all aspects of the breed including the names and addresses of breed clubs in your area, as well as obedience clubs. Inquire about membership.

The American Kennel Club

The American Kennel Club (AKC), devoted to the advancement of purebred dogs, is the oldest and largest registry organization in this country. Every breed recognized by the AKC has a national (parent) club. National clubs are a great source of information on your breed. The affiliated clubs hold AKC events and use AKC rules to hold performance events, dog shows, educational programs, health clinics and training classes. The AKC staff is divided between offices in New York City and Raleigh, North Carolina. The AKC has an excellent Web site that provides information on the organization and all AKC-recognized breeds. The address is www.akc.org.

For registration and performance events information, or for customer service, contact:

THE AMERICAN KENNEL CLUB
5580 Centerview Dr., Suite 200
Raleigh, NC 27606
(919) 233-9767

The AKC's executive offices and the AKC Library (open to the public) are at this address:

THE AMERICAN KENNEL CLUB
260 Madison Ave.
New York, New York 10014
(212) 696-8200 (general information)
(212) 696-8246 (AKC Library)
www.akc.org

UNITED KENNEL CLUB
100 E. Kilgore Rd.
Kalamazoo, MI 49001-5598
(616) 343-9020
www.ukcdogs.com

AMERICAN RARE BREED
ASSOCIATION
9921 Frank Tippett Rd.
Cheltenham, MD 20623
(301) 868-5718 (voice or fax)
www.arba.org

CANADIAN KENNEL CLUB
89 Skyway Ave., Ste. 100
Etobicoke, Ontario
Canada M9W 6R4
(416) 675-5511
www.ckc.ca

ORTHOPEDIC FOUNDATION
FOR ANIMALS (OFA)
2300 E. Nifong Blvd.
Columbia, MO 65201-3856
(314) 442-0418
www.offa.org/

Trainers

Animal Behavior & Training Associates (ABTA)
9018 Balboa Blvd., Ste. 591
Northridge, CA 91325
(800) 795-3294
www.Good-dawg.com

Association of Pet Dog Trainers
(APDT)
(800) PET-DOGS
www.apdt.com

National Association of Dog Obedience
Instructors (NADOI)
729 Grapevine Highway, Ste. 369
Hurst, TX 76054-2085
www.kimberly.uidaho.edu/nadoi

Associations

Delta Society
P.O. Box 1080
Renton, WA 98507-1080
(Promotes the human/animal bond
through pet-assisted therapy and other
programs)
www.petsform.com/DELTASOCIETY/
dsi400.htm

Dog Writers Association of America
(DWAA)
Sally Cooper, Secretary
222 Woodchuck Lane
Harwinton, CT 06791
www.dwaa.org

National Association for Search and
Rescue (NASAR)
4500 Southgate Place, Ste. 100
Chantilly, VA 20157
(703) 222-6277
www.nasar.org

Therapy Dogs International
6 Hilltop Rd.
Mendham, NJ 07945

WEB SITES

General Information—Links to Additional Sites, On-Line Shopping

www.k9web.com – resources for the dog
world

www.netpet.com – pet related products,
software and services

www.apapets.com – The American Pet
Association

www.dogandcatbooks.com – book catalog

www.dogbooks.com – on-line bookshop

www.animal.discovery.com/ – cable
television channel on-line

Health

www.avma.org – American Veterinary
Medical Association (AVMA)

www.avma.org/care4pets/avmaloss.htm
– AVMA site dedicated to consideration of euthanizing sick pets and the
grieving process after losing a pet.

www.aplb.org – Association for Pet Loss
Bereavement (APLB)—contains an
index of national hot lines for on-line
and office counseling.

www.netfopets.com/AskTheExperts.
html – veterinary questions answered.

Breed Information

www.bestdogs.com/news/ – newsgroup

www.cheta.net/connect/canine/breeds/
– Canine Connections Breed
Information Index

91

Activity, 5
Adoption screening process, 7–8
Aging, 35–37
American Kennel Club (AKC), 57, 90
90

Barking, 80–82
Bedding, 11
Bleeding, 27
Breeding standards, 56–63
Broken bones, 28

Chewing, 11, 80–82
Choking, 29
Classifications of dogs, 65
Coat, 60
Coccidiosis, 23
Collars, 11
Confinement, 12–14
Convulsions, 29
Coronavirus, 19
Coughing, 18, 30
Crates, 10–11

Demodetic mange, 26
DHLPP vaccine, 17
Diarrhea, 27–28, 30
Distemper, 18

Ears, 26, 31
Energy, loss of, 30
Euthanasia, 37

First aid, 26–33
Fleas, 23–24
Food
    allergies, 45
    appetite, loss of, 30
    bones, 45–46
    bowls, 11
    dry/moist, 40–42
    free feeding, 44
    growth stages, 39
    schedules, 38, 42–43
    table scraps, 45
    vitamin supplements, 44

Genetic disorders, 33–35
Giardiasis, 23

Grooming
    bathing, 52–54
    brushing, 49–50
    routines, 47
    schedules, 54–55
    supplies, 11, 48
    trimming, 50–51

Head, 31, 57
Health care, 16–17, 19, 88
Heartworm, 22–23
Heatstroke, 28–29
Hepatitis, 18
History, 65–66
Hookworms, 21
Hot/bald spots, 31
Hunting, 6, 63

Identification tags, 11–12
Insect bites, 32

Kennel cough (parainfluenza), 18, 30

Lameness, 30–31
Leashes, 11
Legg-Perthes' disease, 33–34
Leptospirosis, 18–19
Lice, 26
Lumps, 31
Luxating patella, 34

Microchips, 12
Mites, 26
Muzzling, 27

Neutering, 23

Parainfluenza (kennel cough), 18, 30
30
Parasites, 20–26
Parvovirus, 19
Personality
    boldness, 4
    independence, 5–6
    intelligence, 1, 4–5
    socialization, 8, 69
    temperament, 2–3
    tenacity, 3–4
Poisonous substances, 14, 33

Portosystemic shunt, 35
Potty training, 76–80
Preventive health care, 16–17, 19
Progressive retinal atrophy (PRA), 35
35
Protozoans, 23
Puppies, 7–10, 12–14, 30–40

Roundworms, 20–21
Runny nose, 30

Scabies, 26
Shock, 27
Show dogs, 61
Size, 64
Spaying, 23

Tapeworms, 21
Tattoos, 12
Teeth, 31, 34–35
Terriers, history of, 63–64
Therapy Dogs, 91
Ticks, 24–26
Toys, 11–12, 75, 82
Trachea, collapsing, 34
Training
    come command, 82
    follow command, 86–87
    heel command, 85–86
    housetraining, 76–80
    importance, 68
    lure-reward, 71–72, 75, 83
    motivation, 70, 84–85
    owners, 69–70
    play training, 72–73
    potty training, 76–80
    punishment, 73–74
    resources, 88–89
    sit command, 82–83
    trainers, 74, 90–91

Vaccinations, 17–20
Veterinarians, 10, 17
Vomiting, 30, 32–33

Walking, 86–87
Water, 11, 43
Weight, 59–60
Whipworms, 22